Kenji Hodgson | James Nevison

whitecap

The information in this book is true and complete to the best of the authors' knowledge. All recommendations are made without guarantee on the part of the authors or Whitecap Books Ltd. The authors and publisher disclaim any liability in connection with the use of this information.

Note that the inventory at BC Liquor changes constantly. As well, prices change according to demand, currency exchange fluctuations, and other factors. Every effort has been made to ensure prices and vintages were correct at the time of publication.

Edited by Melva McLean
Proofread by Paula Ayer
Cover design by Five Seventeen and Setareh Ashrafologhalai
Interior design and illustrations by Jacqui Thomas
Food icons and occasion icon by Five Seventeen
Additional illustrations (graphs and additional food icons) by Setareh Ashrafologhalai
Typeset by Setareh Ashrafologhalai and Mauve Pagé
Photography by Gerald Deo, James Nevison, and Kenji Hodgson

Printed in Canada

ISBN: 978-1-55285-999-5

Cataloguing data available from Library and Archives Canada.

The publisher acknowledges the financial support of the Government of Canada through the Canada Book Fund (CBF) and the Province of British Columbia through the Book Publishing Tax Credit.

09 10 11 12 13   5 4 3 2 1

contents

preface—the juice

The year 2010 marks the fifth anniversary of the *Had a Glass* series—a fantastic milestone that shows wine drinkers are continuing their quest for great-value wine.

This year also brings change. If you read the cover closely, you have likely already noted the increase in the price spread. Let us explain.

Over the years we have received great feedback on *Had a Glass*. And more and more, we hear a refrain like this: "I've found some great wines in the book, but I'm ready to expand my wine horizons. I'd like to splurge on a bottle. I want to spend more than $20. What about these wines?"

It's true. It's a wide, wide wine world, and even we've been caught crossing the $20 mark. Because we feel there is good-value wine for every earmark, this year we have decided to stretch the budget to encompass those occasions when we're feeling flush.

Now, we need to ensure that we can afford to sip Monday through Friday, and weekends too, so these dearer bottles will stay in the minority. In fact, more than 70 of the 100 wines hold steady at under $20. But there's no denying that value does not heed price tags. You can get bang for your buck between $20 to $30, too. We hope the addition of bottles in this range helps expand your selection of good-value wines.

Other notable additions

Building on our tenet that the good life is a simple matter of embracing good wine, good food, and good people, for 2010 we invited a few friends to share their favourite everyday recipes. The end result is a diverse affair, nicely representative of the variety of characters we always look forward to sharing a glass with.

We also got a little geeky with the new "Charts and Graphs" section, a little visual representation. We break out the rulers and the plotlines for an analysis of *HAG* wines over the last five years: red versus white, country, even bottle closure!

Going local

We continue to see excitement about grapes unique to particular regions. This is not just about Malbec from Argentina and Grüner Veltliner from Austria, two fab varietals that have arguably gone mainstream as wine drinkers have caught on to their allure. We are really impressed with the increasing number of lesser-known indigenous grapes showing up on our shelves. Until recently, these cultivars—the Nero d'Avola of Italy, the Castelão of Portugal, and the Agiorgitiko of Greece—have only been appreciated in their home countries. The fact that they are becoming more widely available bodes well for the wine drinker looking for intriguing new flavours and styles.

Subtle is the new aggro

It's also time to give our taste buds a reprieve! The ultra-ripe, fruit-bomb wines are increasingly heading out of fashion. Sure, there are occasions when these blowhard bottles get the job done. But those occasions are less frequent than the moments when we want a more subtle, nuanced bottle that isn't going to upstage the meal or conversation. The sort of wine that, even when you down a couple glasses (or occasionally a couple more), you still feel all your faculties firing.

Without further ado

And there we have it. Another year, another 100 wines. We are confident that there is a new favourite bottle lurking in the pages of *Had a Glass 2010* for each and every wine drinker. A gold-medal winner, so to speak (and hopefully silver and bronze contenders too), for those just starting to get to know wine as well as for long-time imbibers. Please enjoy!

Sip on,

Kenji & James

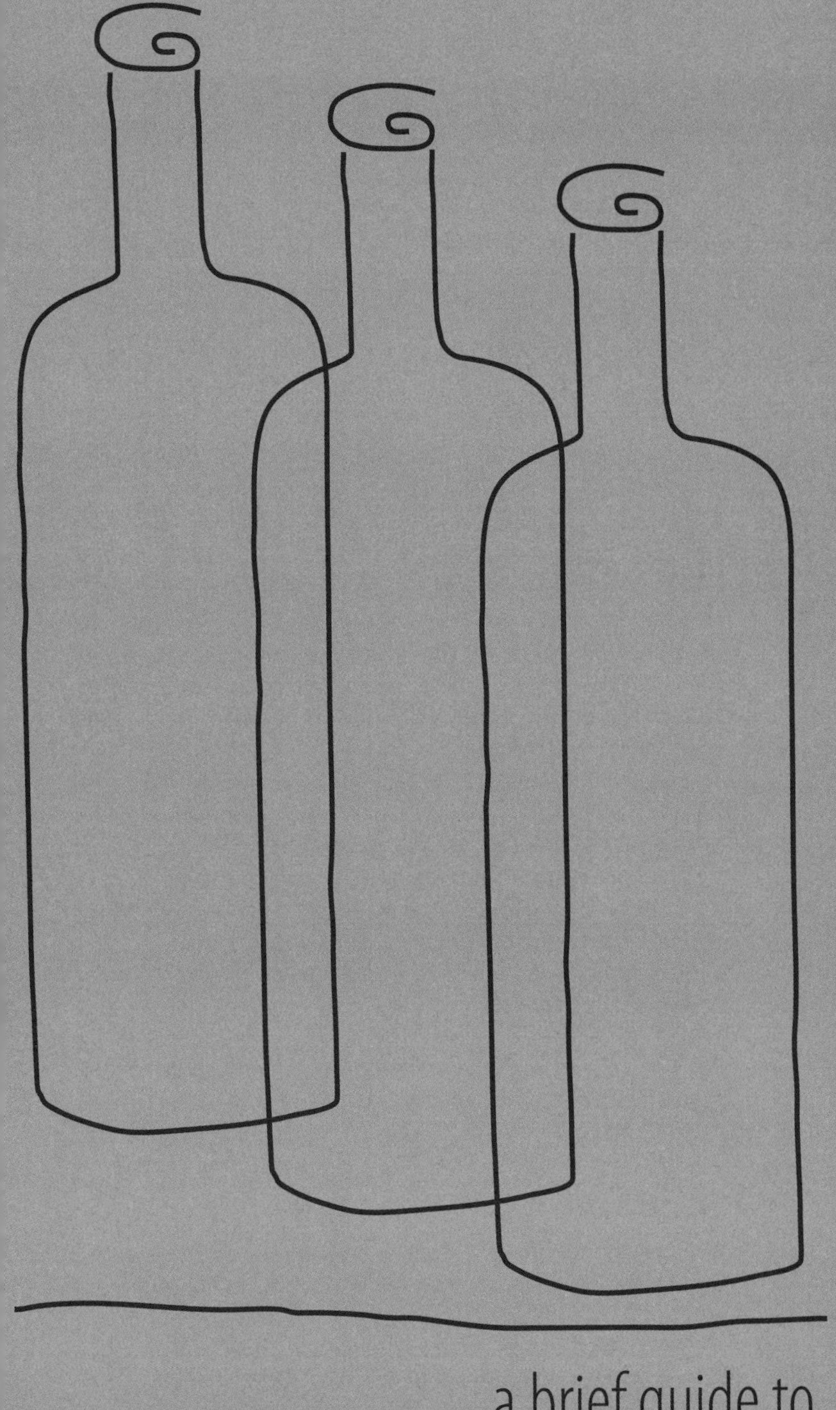

a brief guide to

wine enjoyment

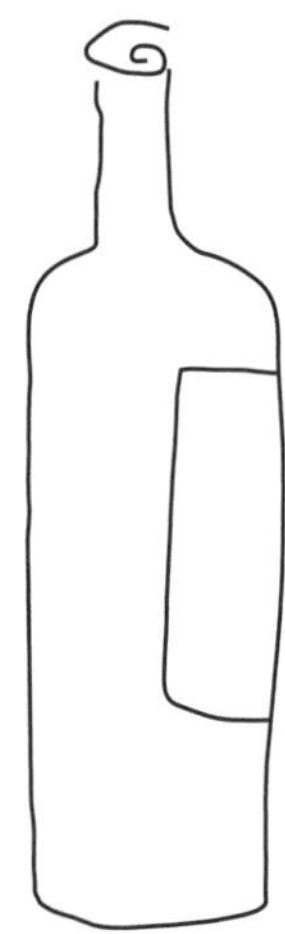

Had a Glass?

Had a Glass gives you the wine goods. In a veritable sea of vinous choice, *Had a Glass* points you in the right direction and makes sure you surface with a good bottle. And it won't cost you big money. Each of the 100 wines in this book checks in at under $30.

Each wine is here for a reason—because it's perfect with a steak, for a picnic, or simply as a stand-alone sipper. And each one is a wine that we personally like to buy and drink.

The wines come from a whole host of countries and are a mix of grape varieties. There are reds and whites, sweets and dries. It's wine diversity we think you'll enjoy.

Pick a page, read the blurb, get the wine, and see what you think. Repeat often.

But remember: Quaffing the grape juice is tons of fun as long as you wine in moderation. Know your limit and always have a designated driver. Such is the path to true wine appreciation.

Buyer Beware

In compiling this list, we've taken care to select wines that are widely available. We all deserve good wine, no matter where we are.

Every effort has been made to ensure prices and vintages were correct at the time of publication. That said, the vagaries of wine buying and copy deadlines conspire against us. The good buys can sell out, and the hot wines could be subject to price increases.

Use this book as a starting point for your wine-buying adventures. Great bottles are out there, and, as with all good hunts, the fun is in the search.

The Value Proposition

"Value" is at best squishy and hard to pin down. Like scoring wine on a 100-point scale, its objective scaffolding tries to prop up a subjective framework. But whether you're after price rollbacks at Wal-Mart or one-of-a-kind designer pieces, true value occurs when rewards exceed expectations.

Here's how value is applied in *Had a Glass*

Most of the time our bank accounts set the upper limit of our wine budget at $20. On occasion we may spend more, but overall we toe the line and once in a while go in for a splurge. From our research, we know most of you feel the same. We all love getting a great $15 bottle of wine. But we love cracking into a tasty $10 bottle even more.

Had a Glass celebrates those wines that give you the best bottle for the buck: the $10 wines that seem like $15, the $15 bottles that stand out, the $20 wines that taste like more, and the $25 bottles that knock your socks off. We see wine as an everyday beverage, not as a luxury—an enjoyable accessory to good living.

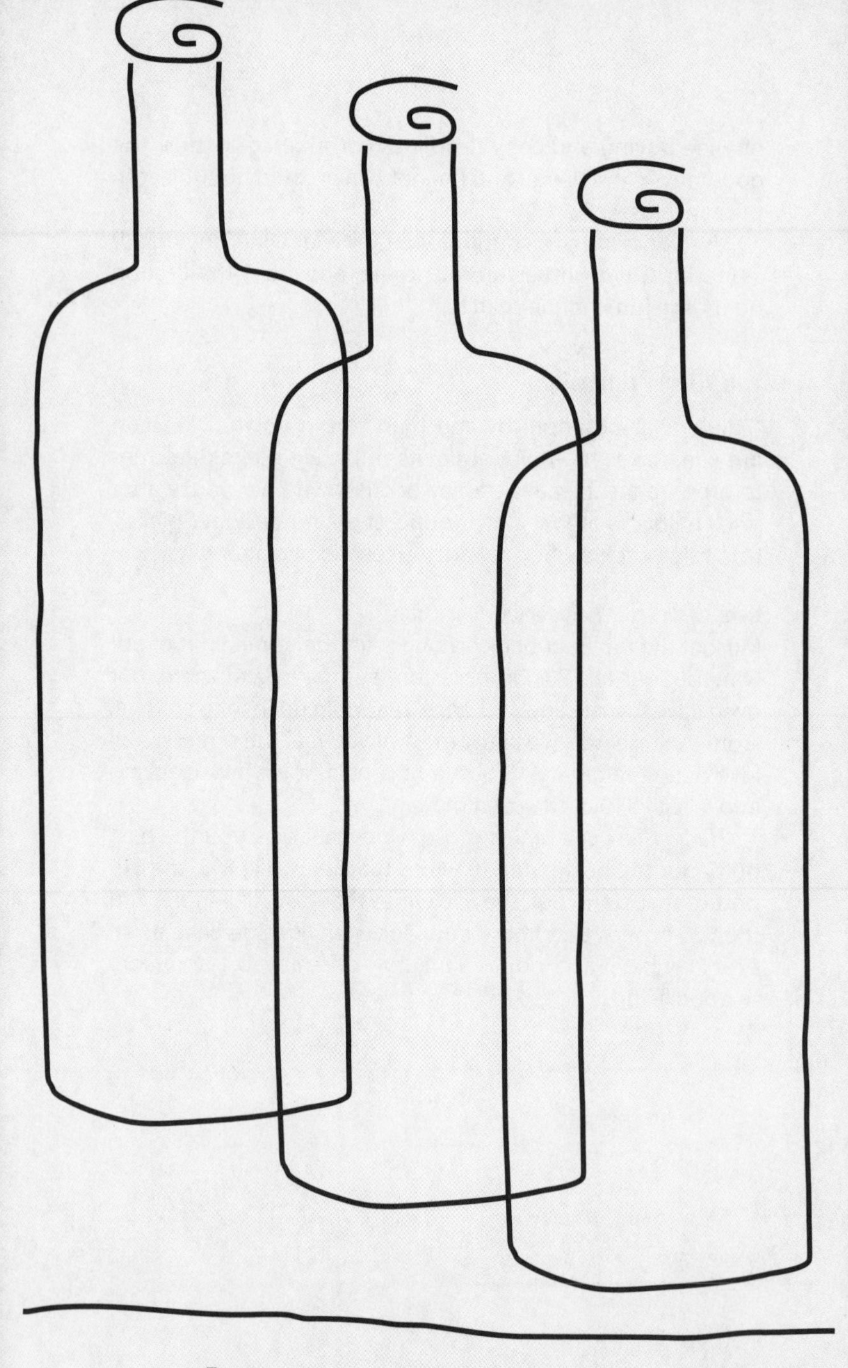

how to taste wine

Drinking wine and tasting wine are two different pastimes. If your only desire is to drink, by all means turn the page and get on to the reviews.

But if you're ready to take your relationship with wine to the next level, it's time to commit to proper tasting technique. It will add to your wine enjoyment as well as permit a complete sensory evaluation of the wine in your glass. We're tired of the philosophy, "A good wine is a wine you like." Sure, at the end of the day, it's a subjective thing where your opinion matters, but what makes a wine good? After you understand how to taste wine, you'll be equipped to make that call.

The Four Steps

Here's the wine-tasting process in four simple steps.

Step 1—The Look

Tilt the wine glass away from you and observe the colour against a white background. Whites can be pallid yellow to deep gold, and reds range from the rich crimson of velvet drapes to the neon of raspberry Kool-Aid. Young white wines may have the brilliant sheen of white gold while older reds often have complex tones of browns superimposed on sombre claret. Whites are typically clear, nearly transparent, whereas a red may be slightly cloudy with sediment.

Step 2—The Swirl

Swirl the wine glass—either on the table or in the air—to draw out the aromas of a wine. Let the wine paint the sides of the glass with long, smooth tears, or legs. Note that these indicate texture and viscosity, not necessarily quality.

Step 3—The Smell

Smelling is wine intimacy. Don't be afraid to put your nose into the glass. A deep inhale will reveal what the wine is about. A wine may have aromas of fruit (melons, berries, cherries), of wood (vanilla or smoke), or of spice (pepper or cloves). You may also get a whiff of less-likely aromas, such as earth, diesel, and leather. Surprising, maybe, but this is what makes wine exciting.

Step 4—The Taste

Take a generous sip of wine. Swirl it in your mouth. The consistency may be thin like skim milk (light-bodied) or it may be thick like cream (full-bodied). Let your tongue taste the different elements of the wine: any sweetness from residual sugars, any tartness from acid, or any bitterness from alcohol. Tannins may dry your gums, making you pucker. Spitting is optional.

Taking Notes

Whether you carry a leather-bound wine journal or scribble on a paper napkin, take wine notes whenever you can. At the very least, jot down the name of the wine and a thumbs-up or thumbs-down beside it. This will save you from repeating the phrase, "I had a great wine last night—I think it had a picture of something on the label."

We use a tasting sheet like this:

TASTING NOTES

TASTING DATE

	WINE 1	WINE 2	WINE 3
WINE NAME • Vintage • Region • Price			
COLOUR • Straw Gold • Claret Purple • Clarity			
SMELL • Fruity • Woody • Spicy • Floral • Earthy			
TASTE • Sweetness • Acidity • Bitterness			
FEEL • Body • Tannin • Finish			
CONCLUSION • Balance • Quality • Do I Like This Wine?			

Usual Aromas

We know that wine smells like wine, but what does wine smell like? There are infinite aromas in fermented grape juice, and everyone smells something different, but here are a few usual aromas to get you started:

Red Wine	White Wine
• Blackberry	• Apple
• Raspberry	• Pear
• Plum	• Peach
• Vanilla	• Grapefruit
• Earth	• Honey

Unusual Aromas

And then there are the weird scents. This is where wine gets interesting. A healthy imagination when tasting wine is always good.

- Barnyard
- Leather chaps
- Wet fur
- Socks
- Ripe cheese

Flights of Fancy

Becoming a good wine taster is all about tasting wines. The more wines you try, the better your frame of reference. A great way to build your database and bolster your tasting skills is to approach wine in "flights." Create a flight by lining up a few wines that share a common theme. Tasting these side by side is like taking three pairs of jeans into the changing room.

Here are a few wine flights to get you started:

Flight 1—Tiers of Côtes du Rhône

Time to step up to the differing-quality wines from the Rhône Valley. Think all Côtes du Rhônes are created equal? Not so! The regulations and designations run strong in this famed wine area. For starters, you have your basic Côtes du Rhône, applicable to a wine region ranging from Vienne to Avignon. The next step up in quality is Côtes du Rhône-Villages, where rules are a little stricter, and berets are a little tighter. Ready to take it to the next level? Then line up a CdR from one of the 19 extra-special villages that get to boast their name on the label, like Rasteau. Is there a difference in taste? See for yourself:

A. Les Brottiers Côtes du Rhône (page 109)

B. Louis Bernard Côtes du Rhône-Villages (page 110)

C. Chapoutier "Rasteau" Côtes du Rhône-Villages (page 126)

Flight 2—Homage to white Bordeaux

The big-three-red blend of Bordeaux—Cabernet Sauvignon, Merlot, and Cabernet Franc—likes to hoard the spotlight. Relegated to second stage is its white grape counterpart, which combines (but is not mutually inclusive of) Sauvignon Blanc, Sémillon, and, to a lesser extent, Muscadelle. Still, it's an elegant style that has found a following around the world, and it's well worth a flight to explore. Check out these three:

A. Trapiche "Astica" Sauvignon Blanc–Sémillon (page 54)

B. 1st fleet Sémillon–Sauvignon Blanc (page 63)

C. Dourthe "Dourthe No. 1" Bordeaux White (page 67)

Flight 3—Bring on the bubble

Oh, the joys of sparkling wine! A top contender for most versatile style, sparkling wine goes gangbusters with almost any meal and is our top choice for wine any hour of the day: at brunch, lunch, or a midnight toast. The best way to appreciate the unique styles and flavours of the various sparkling wines made around the world is to line them up all in one tasting. Try popping these corks together:

A. Codorníu "Classico" Cava Brut (page 146)

B. Mionetto (page 147)

C. Gloria Ferrer (page 149)

Self-Help for Wine Monotony

If your wining has been monotonous of late, try these wine-buying strategies and never be stuck on the same bottle again.

Branching out

When you find yourself smitten by a particular grape—say, perhaps, the moody Malbec or voluptuous Viognier—expand on your infatuation by exploring similar bottles from around the wine world.

Riesling ranks right up there at the top of the notable grapes list, celebrated by wine drinkers around the globe. This year the Riesling selection traverses both Old and New Worlds. Germany is the undisputed heavyweight of the Riesling regions, so check out the BEX (page 70) and Dr. L (page 75) for some classic Riesling flavours. Then traipse across the Atlantic back home to Canada. Our cooler-climate wine country gets compared to Germany's, so it's no surprise that Riesling has made a home for itself here as well. Ontario gets represented with Cave Spring (page 73), while B.C. weighs in with Tantalus (page 82).

Love of the land

Certain parts of the world make certain types of wine. This is often indicated on the bottle by appellation, or where the wine originated. Flipping through the pages this year, you'll see some great wine locales, such as Mosel and McLaren Vale. If you like the wine of a particular appellation, try others from the same locale.

For a better look at northern Italy's crisp whites, which rose to fashionable wine fame in the 1980s, check out the zingy finesse of the Araldica Cortese (page 64). If the current trends roaming the streets are any indication, it's time for a revival! Next, crack open the delectable Principessa Gavia (page 83), which bigups the reputation of the Gavi region, and is made entirely from the Cortese grape, too.

Trading up

A winery commonly makes different tiers of wines—the Toyota and the Lexus. *Had a Glass* is all about the Toyotas, but if you like what you're test-driving, look for the luxury version.

Penfolds is a major Australian winery with bottles available across the entire price spectrum. We find their Thomas Hyland Shiraz (page 129) a particularly tasty value, but there's no denying that collectors around the world go gaga for their flagship red—and one of the world's iconic bottles—Penfolds's Grange. Of course, the Grange will set you back about 25 times as much as the Hyland, but it's one of those wines you leave in your cellar to share with your as-yet-unborn kids two decades down the road (or even with the grandkids 40 or 50 years later!). In between the two we've found spectacular Shiraz taste in Penfolds's Bin 28 (about $40) and St. Henri (around $65).

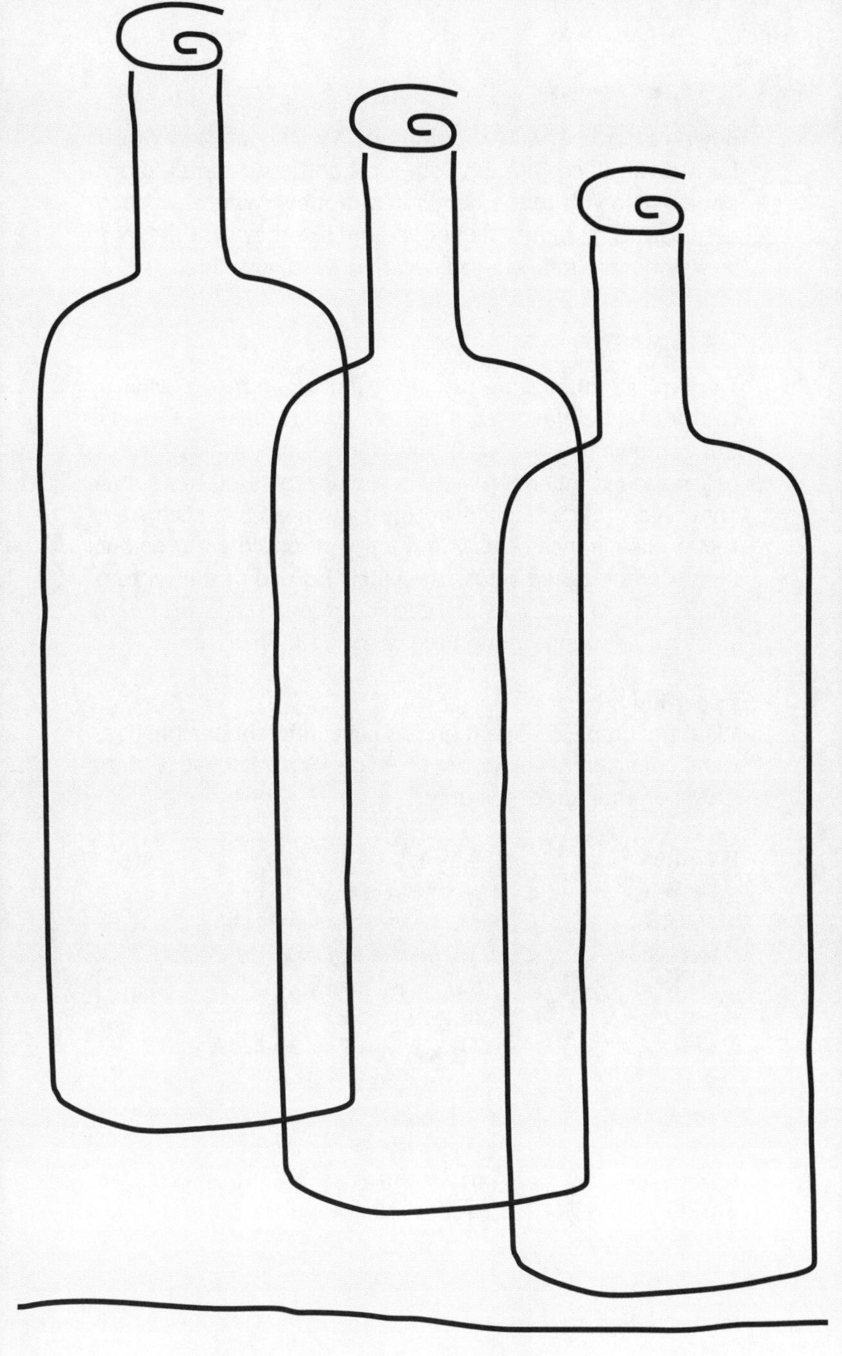

how to buy wine

Buying a bottle of wine shouldn't raise your heart rate. Wine is fun, and strolling through your local bottle shop should be a joy. It isn't a visit to the dentist. But not everyone feels confident to strut through the liquor store like they own the joint, so we offer the following advice on how to buy wine.

Get Organized

The typical liquor store or wine shop organizes its wine by country—a helpful categorical tool if you're feeling regional, but somewhat awkward if you want a Merlot and have to run around comparing one geographical offering to another. Things can get particularly unruly if you head to an Old World section like France or Italy and are confronted with regional names emblazoned across the labels instead of the types of grape. Get to know where certain grapes come from, and you'll be sleuthing through the bottle aisles in no time.

GrapeWHAT

What the grape? Different grapes have different personalities. Here, in five words or so, are the typical characteristics of the most common grape varieties.

Whites	
Chardonnay	apple, dry, often oaked, omnipresent
Chenin Blanc	green apple, steely, good acidity
Gewürztraminer	rich but refreshing, spicy, tropical
Pinot Blanc	fresh, fruity, mild, drink young
Pinot Gris	versatile, aromatic, honey
Pinot Grigio	same grape but Italian-style and crisp
Riesling	dry to sweet, good acidity, racy
Sauvignon Blanc	gooseberry, grassy, crisp, light
Sémillon	lean or luscious, Tupperware, honey
Torrontés	fresh, light, dry, floral
Viognier	trendy, floral, soft but peppy

Reds	
Cabernet Franc	raspberry, bell pepper
Cabernet Sauvignon	king grape, tannic, full, ages well
Carmenère	herbaceous, dark fruit, unique
Gamay	cherry, medium weight
Grenache	strawberry, bit rustic, potent
Malbec	plum, powerful, tannin
Merlot	approachable, smooth, full, dark fruit
Pinotage	South Africa, berry, spice
Pinot Noir	cherry, forest floor, soft tannins
Sangiovese	cherry, earthy, good acidity
Shiraz	medium, peppery, powerful, lotsa fruit
Syrah	same grape but less fruit, more earth
Tempranillo	juicy or dense, cherry or blackberry
Zinfandel	strawberry pie, brambles, jammy

GrapeWHERE

You're in a wine shop, standing in front of the Italy section, but the label just isn't telling you anything. What happened to Chardonnay and Merlot? It's a long story, but in the meantime here's the lowdown on what goes into some wines named by place.

Whites	
Bordeaux, France	Sémillon, Sauvignon Blanc
Burgundy, France	Chardonnay
Côtes du Rhône, France	Viognier, Roussanne, Marsanne, and others
Gavi, Italy	Cortese
Muscadet Sèvre et Maine	Melon de Bourgogne
Champagne, France	Chardonnay, Pinot Noir, Pinot Meunier

Reds	
Bordeaux, France	Cabernet Sauvignon, Merlot, Cab Franc
Burgundy, France	Pinot Noir
Beaujolais, France	Gamay
Côtes du Rhône, France	Syrah, Grenache, and others
Cahors, France	Malbec
Chianti, Italy	Sangiovese
Valpolicella, Italy	Corvina
Rioja, Spain	Tempranillo, Garnacha

Occasional Wine

Of course, regardless of how the wines are organized, we're often there to buy a wine for a certain occasion, be it to go with Mom's meatloaf or to celebrate Jane's birthday. This is a logical way to buy wine, especially—excuse us—for the occasional wine drinker. It's the time-honoured question: Do you match the wine to the food or match the food to the wine? The answer will affect your wine-buying decision.

GrapeWHEN

Matching wines to food is like accessorizing an outfit. You want everything to go together, but that doesn't mean you have to be obvious. And there are bonus points for creativity.

Whites	
Chardonnay	chicken, crab
Chenin Blanc	snapper, salad
Gewürztraminer	curry, Asian
Pinot Blanc	goat cheese, veggie soup
Pinot Gris	halibut, smoked salmon
Riesling	turkey, applesauce
Sauvignon Blanc	shellfish, fish
Sémillon	prawns, pork
Torrontés	aperitif, carrot soup
Viognier	grilled fish, ginger
Champagne	in the bath with mango and a friend

Reds	
Cabernet Franc	roast, goulash
Cabernet Sauvignon	steak, kebabs
Carmenère	alone, late at night
Gamay	nachos
Malbec	slow-grilled food, stuffed cabbage
Merlot	Camembert, mushrooms
Pinotage	pork, game
Pinot Noir	salmon, duck
Sangiovese	pizza, pasta
Shiraz	BBQ
Tempranillo	bacon, beef stir-fry
Zinfandel	nachos, teriyaki
Port	with a book

Feelings, Nothing More Than Feelings

There's nothing better than matching wines to mood, and often when we find ourselves staring at a wall of wine wondering what to put in the basket, a simple mood check serves to stimulate the purchasing process. A bold evening often calls for an aggressive wine, just as a mellow affair requires an equally subdued bottle. Feeling adventurous? Experiment with a new, never-before-tasted wine. Looking for a little comfort? Head back to the tried-and-true.

FEELING	TRY	FROM
Bold/Aggressive	Shiraz	Australia/B.C.
Mellow/Chill	Pinot Noir	France/California
Sophisticated	Cabernet Blend	Chile
Edgy	Riesling	Germany/Australia
Ambivalent	Chardonnay	Anywhere

Expanding Your Wine Horizons

And while we're still on the topic of feelings . . . If you're feeling a bit adventurous, now is the perfect time to experiment with a never-before-tasted wine.

LIKE	TRY	FROM
Cabernet Sauvignon	Tempranillo	Spain
Shiraz	Côtes du Rhône	France
Merlot	Malbec	Argentina
Chardonnay	Pinot Gris	B.C.
Sauvignon Blanc	Grüner Veltliner	Austria

Required Reading

What appears on the wine label counts. You can learn a lot about a wine before you buy. The trick is to know what's worth reading. Wine label literacy can go a long way towards increasing wine enjoyment and decreasing buyer remorse.

Old World

New World

Wine or winery name

Back in the day, the name would be that of a chateau or domaine, or possibly it'd be a proprietary name that was used by a winemaking co-operative. While these are still out there, now brand names, animal species, and hip monikers are gracing wine bottles, all in an effort to help you remember what you drank.

Vintage

The year printed on the label is the year the grapes were grown. There are good years and bad years, usually determined by weather conditions. Should you care? In good grape-weather years there'll be more good wine, but off years don't necessarily mean bad wine. If the winemakers know what they're doing, their wines should be able to overcome the less-than-perfect vintages. A vintage also tells you how old the wine is. Oldies are not necessarily goodies, but many wines will improve with cellar time (see "Mixed half-case," page 29).

We include the vintages for the wines we review. Where no vintage is listed, the wine is "non-vintage," meaning it's been made from a mix of years.

Alcohol

Generally expressed as "alcohol by volume" (ABV), this tells you how much wine you can taste before the line between "tasting" and "drinking" becomes blurred. Or blurry. As a rough guide, higher alcohol content (14 percent is high, anything above 14.5 percent is really high) suggests a heftier, more intense wine. On the other side of the ABV spectrum, wines with less than 11 percent will often be off-dry (slightly sweet). High alcohol doesn't connote a better wine. Regardless of the number, if the wine is without the grating bitterness of alcohol—not tasting like a vodka shot—then it's a well-balanced drop.

Appellation

Or, where the grapes came from. Old World wine, say from France, often gives you the appellation instead of the grape variety. You'll see something like "Bordeaux," which describes where the grapes originated, but because French laws state only certain grapes are authorized in certain areas, the appellation name also hints at what grapes made the wine. So, appellations (Burgundy, Chianti, Rioja) define taste.

Grape variety

You pick up a can of soup and it's "mushroom" or "tomato." On a wine bottle you often see the wine variety: Shiraz or Merlot or Chardonnay, to mention a few. These are your "single varietal" wines, as opposed to "blended" wines, the likes of Cabernet-Merlot and Sémillon–Sauvignon Blanc. Keep in mind that single varietal wines are no better than blends, and vice versa. Trust your taste buds.

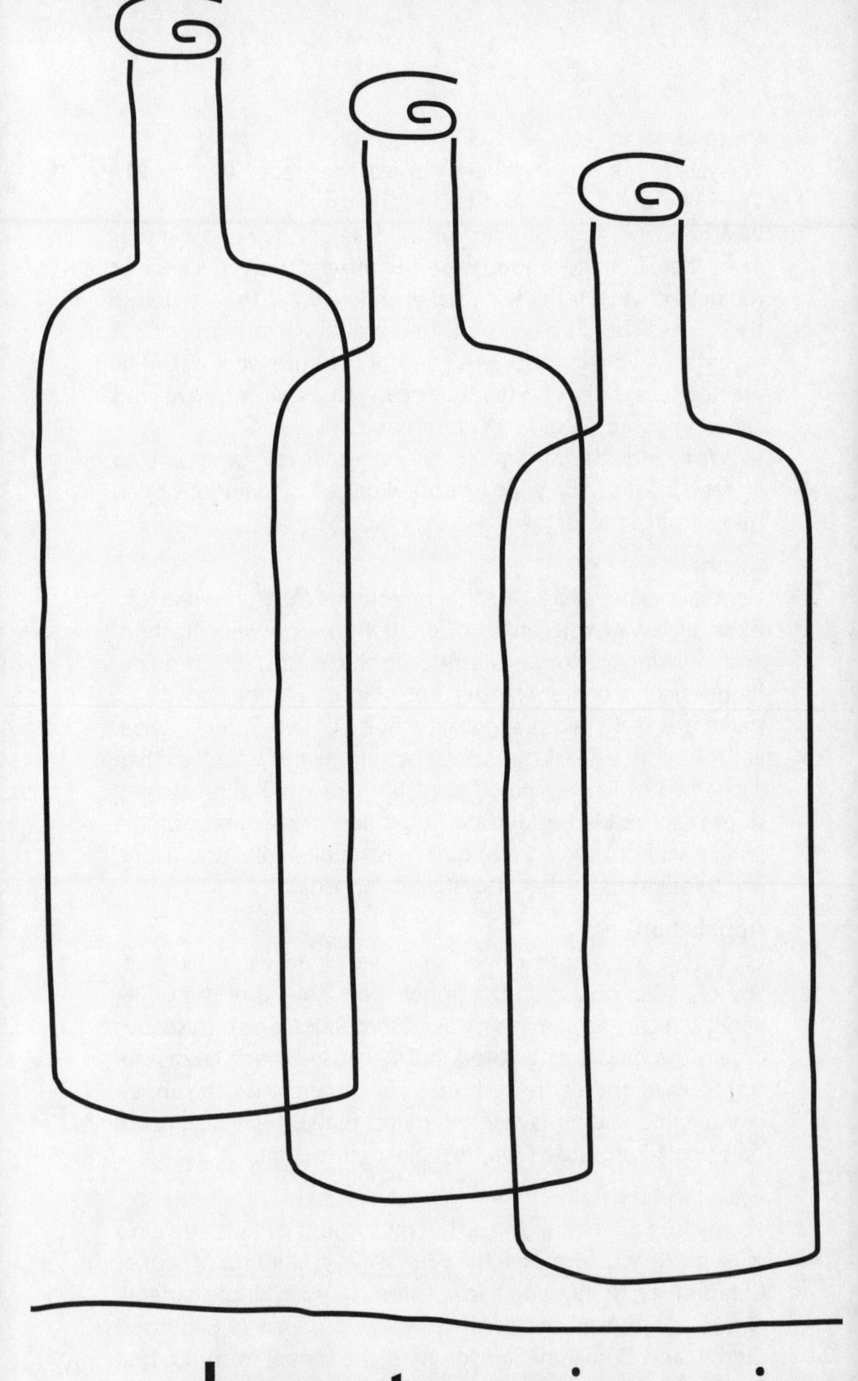

how to enjoy wine

Glasses and Stemware

Not all wine glasses are created equal, though drinking wine from any glass can be enjoyable. Allow us to explain.

Wine is like golf. There's an infinite array of specialized accessories, but all you really need to play the game is a set of clubs. Likewise, all your wine requires is a glass. It's up to you to decide how much you want to invest and how involved you want to get. Just don't tell us you can't drink wine because you don't have a wineglass.

There are benefits to good stemware:

- Swirling wine in the larger bowl common to fancy glasses does wonders for a wine's aromas. Pouring a few fingers at a time lets you get a proper swirl going.
- Holding the stem helps to keep white wines chilled and grubby fingerprints off the glass.
- There's no denying the elegant tactile sensation of a thin rim caressing the lips.

We use a motley collection of crystal we've collected over the years as well as a cupboardful of everyday tumblers for backyard bashes.

Decanters

After glasses, the next most important wine accessory is the decanter. A secret to wine enjoyment, the decanter can do more for your wines than you can imagine. Decanting old wines to remove the liquid from the sediment will keep your teeth clean, but how many of us drink old wines these days?

Use your decanter to decant young wines, letting them breathe. Most wines we buy are made to be drunk young—often too young—and decanting will open these wines up, revealing their character. Your decanter is a wine time machine; don't be afraid to shake it.

Anything can be used as a decanter, from a clean teapot to a water jug. To get serious about your decanter, look for a glass container with a wide base and a narrow opening. This facilitates swirling, makes for easier pouring—and looks pretty sexy.

Corkscrews

We've been to our share of dinner parties where the main event was getting the cork out of the bottle, usually at the mercy of an antediluvian Butterfly corkscrew.

We think it would be a better wine world if everyone's knife drawer also had a Waiter's Friend. They're cheap (you can find them under $10) and effective (never yet met a cork it couldn't beat), and make you look like you mean wine business when looped around your belt.

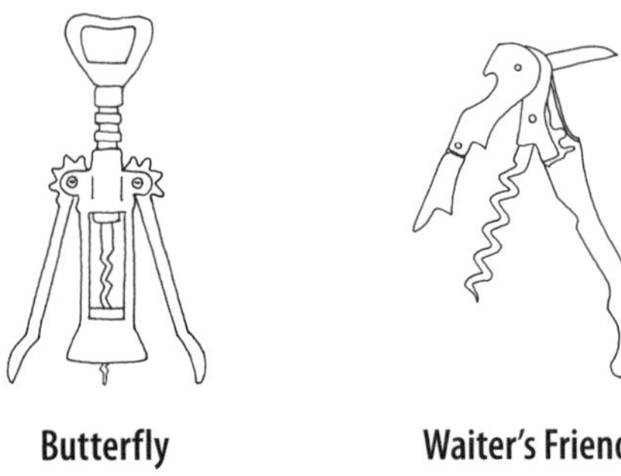

Butterfly **Waiter's Friend**

Storing and Aging Your Wine

We don't mean to come across like we're down on wine cellars—quite the opposite. There's nothing we like better than rummaging around dusty wine racks sticky with cobwebs. But there's wine for aging and there's wine for drinking, and this book is about the latter.

In fact, over 90 percent of the wine sold today is made for drinking now, and to drink a wine now, you don't need a cellar. But, they say—and we've tasted proof—that wine changes as it gets older, hence the concept of storing wine.

Do you need a cellar or a Sub-Zero? For most wine, the answer is "no." Display your wine in that IKEA wine rack, stash it in the cupboard, or keep it handy under your bed.

Mixed half-case

There's a handful of wines in this book that you could have fun with by letting them age for a few years. Put them in a box, put the box on its side, and hide it in a closet.

1) Tantalus Riesling (page 82)
2) Loimer "Lois" Grüner Veltliner (page 79)
3) Tinhorn Creek "Oldfield's Collection" Merlot (page 143)
4) Chono "Reserva" Syrah (page 117)
5) Penfolds "Thomas Hyland" Shiraz (page 129)
6) Ceuso Scurati "Sicilia" (page 132)

Wine Handling

Serving temperatures

Red wine	18°C (65°F) *a bit below room temperature*
White (and rosé) wine	10°C (50°F) *20 minutes out of the fridge*
Sparkling and sweet wine	5°C (40°F) *straight from the fridge*

Tips

- Err on the side of serving a wine too cold. The bottle will always warm up as it sits on the table.
- If a wine is too sweet, serving it cold will make it taste drier.
- All dessert wine should be served at fridge temperature, unless it's red—like port—in which case serve it at the same temperature as red wine.

Leftovers

Once a bottle is opened, how long do you have to drink it? It's true that wine starts to deteriorate once it's exposed to oxygen, but finishing a bottle the following day—or if you must, even the day after—is fine.

Sure, there are tricks. Put the open bottle in the fridge, whether white or red, to slow down the oxidization, or use a vacuum pump to remove oxygen from the bottle, or buy spray bottles filled with inert gas to blanket the wine and protect it against oxygen, or drop marbles into the bottle to displace the air.

But if you ask us, you're better off breaking out a chunk of cheese and polishing off the wine.

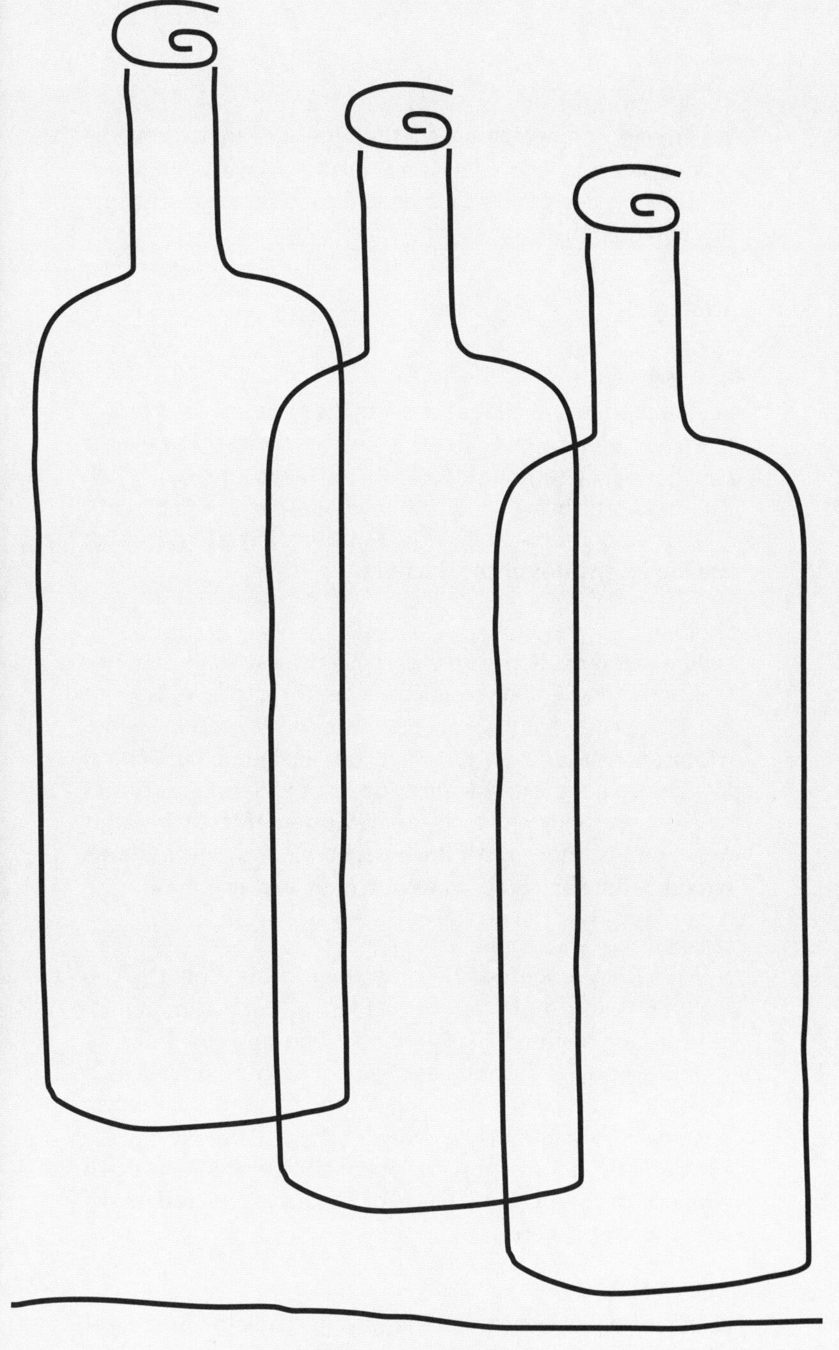

food and wine

We prepare our meals to match the wine we want to drink. We order a steak only if we feel like drinking red wine. But, we've been told, some people decide on what they're going to eat first and then think about what wine to have.

Strategies

Red meat

Red wine. There are a lot of wine myths out there, and half of them are Grade "A" bull. "Red wine with red meat," however, is true. Besides synchronizing colours, red meat is hearty. It's full-flavoured and heavy, and red wines—especially Cabernets, Merlots, and Syrahs—follow the same lines. **Strategy: Match the big intensities of the flavours.**

Shellfish

Light, white wine. There are even white wines, like fino sherry, that taste briny. Could you ask for a better match? We also bet on white wines that have no, or little, oak flavour. These wines will taste fresh, just how you want your shellfish to be. Of note, Rieslings (a good example on page 73) and Sauvignon Blancs (page 68) are tangy with crisp acidity. **Strategy: Match the lightness and freshness of the flavours. Bonus strategy: If there's lemon or lime involved, wine with high acidity is good.**

Salmon

Medium white or lighter red wine. "Salmon steak" should tip you off. It's fish, sure, but if you've ever had a spring salmon flopping around on the deck of your boat, you know the fish is no shrimp. Good B.C. salmon has plenty of flavour, and it takes a wine with extra heft to get along with it. White-wise, try oaked or unoaked Chardonnays. Red-wise, try a Pinot Noir (page 136). And don't forget rosé (page 88). **Strategy: Match a rich white with the rich omega-3s of salmon; if it's red, make sure the tannins are soft.**

White fish

Light to medium white wine. The way you cook the fish makes all the difference. The delicacy of a poached fish needs a delicate wine, like Gavi (page 83) or Pinot Blanc (page 60). If you're baking, opt for a bit of thickness from a white Bordeaux blend (page 67) or a Pinot Grigio (page 66). Frying in a glorious sea of butter? Open a Chardonnay or a sparkling wine (page 145). **Strategy: The oilier the fish, the heavier your wine can be.**

Pork

Medium to full whites; light to medium reds. The "other" white meat can take to a lot of different wines. We love a good, off-dry Riesling (page 75) if there's a German flair to your cooking (read: applesauce); we love an Italian red (page 108) if it's a pot roast. **Strategy: You can definitely put grapes before pigs. Pork is highly wine-friendly—it's all to do with how you sauce it.**

Chicken

Medium white wine. Everyone likes chicken, right? And likewise, everyone's happy with a medium-bodied, dry white wine. How can you go wrong? This is the perfect combo to serve your date the first time you cook for them. Unless they're vegetarian. Then serve pasta alfredo. Unless they're vegan. Then serve tofu. Anyway, a Sémillon works (page 65), and if you want to get creative, try a bubbly. **Strategy: Hard to go wrong with white wine and chicken. It can work with cream sauce or tofu as well.**

Spicy

Fruity, off-dry white wine. Putting wine against spice is like pitting the Dukes of Hazzard against the A-Team. We pity the fool! In mild doses, a slightly sweet, fruity wine like Gewürztraminer (page 81) or an aromatic white blend (page 71) will show through spice, but if it's heavy jalapeño, go beer. **Strategy: Get a white wine that has more flavour than the dish has spice.**

Heavy sauce

White or medium red. We learned the definition of "heavy sauce" in Paris: cream and butter, baby. It challenges wine pairing because whatever you put the sauce on tastes a lot like the sauce. If it's classic roux, a white like Burgundy (page 78) or a soft, medium red (like the Gamay on page 111) works. **Strategy: Prevent cardiac arrest with some polyphenols and a walk around the block after dinner.**

Dessert

Red or white wine that's sweeter than the dessert. If the wine is too dry, the sweet dessert will make it seem even drier, and that's just way too dry for us. Both the Hardys "Whiskers Blake" Classic Tawny (page 158) and the Dow's Late Bottled Vintage Port (page 157) are sweet but not cloying, and this is why they rock. People seem to like dry red wine with chocolate. Here, make sure your red wine is full-flavoured and not too tannic, like a Merlot. **Strategy: Late harvest, ice wine, port, sweet sherry, Madeira. This is your arsenal.**

Cheese

Try anything. It won't hurt. A wine salesperson once told us, "If you want to sell wine, serve cheese." The magical mud called cheese makes everything taste good. We highly recommend it before dinner, during dinner, and definitely after dinner. Creamy cheese is tasty with a creamy wine like the Township 7 (page 80), hard cheese with a solid wine like the Amalaya de Colomé Tinto (page 124). A beautiful match is blue cheese and dessert wine (page 155). **Strategy: You'll always run out of cheese, so stock up.**

Icons

These icons will reappear in our list of top wines. Note that the index starting on page 164 organizes the wines in this book by the food matches we recommend.

Food icons

Wine and food together is gastronomy in stereo. To help your pairings sing, here are some general guidelines:

BEEF
Big protein: roast, steak, stew

CHEESE
Hard or soft, stinky or mild

DESSERT
And other sweets

EGGS

FISH
Trout, salmon, halibut, tuna

LAMB
The other red meat

ON ITS OWN

PORK
Chops, kebabs, loin

POULTRY
Turkey, chicken, duck, guinea fowl

SHELLFISH
Bi-valves, oh my!: oysters, mussels, clams

SPICY
Szechuan, mild curry, Thai

VEGETARIAN
Tofu-friendly: stir-fries, ratatouille, mushrooms galore

Occasion icons

Wine is tied to experience. There's a wine for every occasion, but certain times call for specific wines. Whether the moment is casual or formal, serious or celebratory, a glass of wine can match the mood.

APERITIF
Suitable pre-meal to get the gastro-juices flowing

BEGINNER
Easy to drink, varietally true wines

BYO
Crowd-pleasers; wines to pack along

CELLAR
Wines that get better after a couple of years

PATIO/PICNIC
Hot-weather sipping wines

ROCK OUT
Wines to let your hair down, tussle that do, and coif that mullet

ROMANCE
Wines to get busy with

WEDNESDAY WINE
To get you through the mid-week hump

WINE GEEK
Wines on the esoteric side that only a geek could love

WINTER WARMER
Wines to ward off any chill

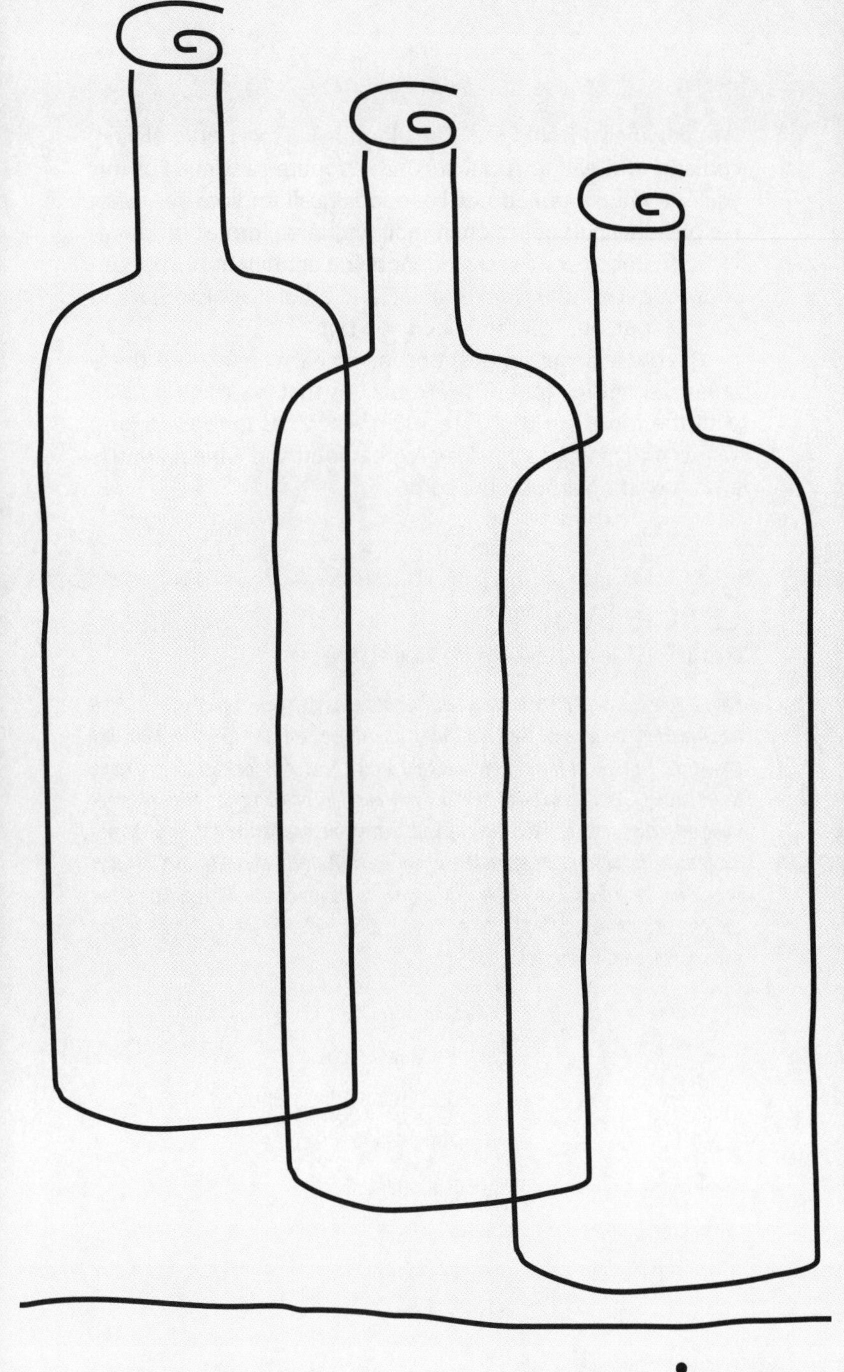

recipes

What's wine without food? The ultimate foil to a bottle of vino, cooking and eating is our second-favourite pastime. For this year's book we polled our best-cooking friends to see what recipes they had going on in their kitchens. From sublime ceviche to knock-your-socks-off vindaloo, a brilliant black bean soup, super-simple clam linguini, and a bouillabaisse packed with flavour, our comrades came up big.

Of course, wine suggestions follow each recipe, but these are never set in stone. They're bottles that we think go well with the food, but there are 100 great wines in these pages, so mix and match as you like. A great food and wine pairing is always waiting around the corner.

Ceviche by Steve

prep time 15 minutes | **cooking time** 3 hours | **serves** 4

Long before we were privy to things of culinary consequence—when slow cooking happened only because we were fumbling with a recipe, and olive oil was just another non-stick device—our friend Steve was light years ahead of us (at least when it came to the kitchen). We'd show up at a potluck with our chips and dip, and he'd have something perfectly tataki-ed. We'd show up with a casserole, and he'd be dishing up homemade ravioli in mascarpone sauce. Likely he'd been milking the Milanese cows just days prior. Here, Steve divulges his triple-fish-and-scallop house ceviche. He reminds us that the leftover marinade, called "leche de tigre," is rumoured to be either a hangover cure or an aphrodisiac. You make the call.

¾ lb (375 g)	fresh white fish (snapper, cod, halibut)
	handful of bay scallops
1	hot pepper (serrano, habañero, etc.)
½	red onion, sliced
1	clove garlic, minced
⅓ cup (80 mL)	lime juice
3 Tbsp (45 mL)	pineapple juice
	splash of orange juice

1 Tbsp (15 mL)	olive oil
	handful of chopped fresh cilantro
	pinch of salt

1 Cut the fish into ¼-inch (6 mm) cubes and place in a glass dish along with the scallops.
2 Remove the seeds from the pepper, unless you love the heat, and slice thinly. Toss the pepper slices, onion, and garlic with the fish.
3 Pour the lime, pineapple, and orange juices over the mixture. Lightly toss the ingredients together to coat. Cover with plastic kitchen wrap and place in the refrigerator for 2 to 3 hours. (The fish will begin to turn opaque as it marinates.)
4 Before serving, lightly fold in the olive oil, cilantro, and salt.
5 Serve ceviche on top of a leaf of butter lettuce, accompanied by oven-roasted yam rounds and corn on the cob, or in a martini glass with tortilla chips.

What to Drink

Sparkling wine goes with everything, and ceviche is no exception. In fact, Steve's rendition here may just be the ultimate partner for bubble, especially Codorníu's Brut (page 146). For a non-fizzy alternative, try Peller Estates's snappy Pinot Blanc (page 60).

Pat's Clam Linguini

prep time 10 minutes | **cooking time** 15 minutes | **serves** 2

Most of us have a friend or two who've decamped from the comforts of Canada to go live in a foreign country. And most of us envy them every step of the way. Pat and her copain trekked off to France last year. They first settled in Toulouse and now inhabit the wilds of Paris. We asked Pat what dish she used to make when she lived in Vancouver, before she entered the world of daily open-air markets, unpasteurized cheese, and Beaujolais at lunch.

½ lb (250 g)	linguini (dried)
2 Tbsp (30 mL)	olive oil
1	small onion, finely diced

3	cloves garlic, thinly sliced
½ cup (125 mL)	white wine
	handful of cherry tomatoes, halved
5 oz (142 g)	can baby clams in nectar
	pinch of dried chili flakes
	grated Parmigiano Reggiano cheese
¼ cup (60 mL)	chopped flat-leaf parsley

1 Cook the linguini in boiling salted water until al dente.
2 Heat the oil in a saucepan over medium-high heat. Sauté the onion and garlic until the onion is soft and translucent but not browned, about 5 to 7 minutes.
3 Add the wine, tomatoes, clams (with their nectar), and chili flakes and boil for about 5 minutes, or until the liquid is reduced by one-third.
4 Add the cooked linguini and the Parmigiano Reggiano to the sauce, turning the pasta to coat.
5 Serve with parsley sprinkled overtop.
6 Garlic bread and lemon wedges as garnish are a nice touch.

What to Drink

The vinous foil to this dish is any bottle with so much polish you can barely tell you're drinking it. Not that it should be something insipid; in fact, quite the opposite. Look for a wine boasting brilliant freshness and purity of flavour, but with a balance that allows the beautifully flavoured sauce to shine. We're going Château de Chasseloir's Muscadet (page 77) or the Principessa Gavia (page 83). Or both.

Janey's Go-To Coconut and Black Bean Soup

prep time 30 minutes | **cooking time** 60 minutes | **serves** 4

Our friend Janey offered to contribute a second time to the pages of our wine musings. Her first piece was the pivotal foreword to the original Have a Glass *wine guide, circa*

2003 (this was even before the first Had a Glass *in 2006). Years later, and to much acclamation, she returns with a delicious and yet oh-so-simple recipe for a soup that can easily be a starter for a multi-course meal or the main event at lunch. All you have to do is add some bread and a wedge of cheese.*

1 Tbsp (30 mL)	vegetable oil
1	medium onion, chopped
2	ribs celery, chopped
1 tsp (5 mL)	cumin seeds
2	cloves garlic, peeled
	juice of 1 lime
¼–½ tsp (1–2 mL)	cayenne pepper
two 14 oz (398 mL)	cans black beans
1 cup (250 mL)	coconut milk
2 cups (500 mL)	vegetable stock (or water)
1 cup (250 mL)	frozen corn (optional)
½ cup (125 mL)	diced red pepper (optional)
½ cup (125 mL)	diced tomato (optional)
	salt and pepper
1	lime, cut into wedges
	handful of fresh cilantro, chopped

1. Heat the vegetable oil in a saucepan. Sauté the onion and celery on medium-low heat until they are translucent.
2. Grind the cumin with a mortar and pestle or spice grinder, then add the garlic and grind further.
3. Add the lime juice and cayenne pepper to the mortar or spice grinder and mix. Add to the pan. Continue to sauté for about 5 minutes, until the mixture browns slightly.
4. Add the black beans (including the liquid from the can), coconut milk, and stock or water.
5. Bring to a boil, then reduce heat and simmer for 20 minutes.
6. Blend the soup with an immersion blender, or put about half the soup in a regular blender and blend until smooth, then recombine.

7 Add the frozen corn, diced red pepper, and diced tomato, if using.

8 Return to a simmer. Season with salt and pepper to taste. Garnish with lime wedges and fresh cilantro.

What to Drink

A great midday dish calls for a great midday wine, and we can't think of a better afternoon tipple than Pinot Gris (or Grigio, *mio amico*). The ones we'd call from the bullpen are Dunavar's seriously sippable rendition (page 55), or Bollini's take, if you want something more serious (page 72).

Cawston Chicken Bouillabaisse

prep time 20 minutes | **cooking time** 90 minutes | **serves** 4

We don't really get the term "foodie." Is this a compliment? We'd do a double take if someone called us "wine-ies." And we'd take full offence if it happened to come out as "weenies." So when we refer to our friends Rhys and Alishan we make doubly sure to call them by their rightly earned sobriquets, les personnes gastronomiques. *We make sure to enunciate very carefully. Anyway, these two foodies passed on this ridiculously divine turf-themed bouillabaisse, a simplified adaptation of Ina Garten's version. It's outstandingly easy to whip up, and the flavours well exceed the effort.*

The Bouillabaisse

½ tsp (2 mL)	saffron
1	whole chicken, cut into pieces
1 Tbsp (15 mL)	chopped fresh rosemary leaves
	salt and pepper
2 Tbsp (30 mL)	olive oil
3–4	cloves garlic, peeled and chopped
1	bay leaf
1 tsp (5 mL)	fennel seeds
	grated orange zest (from half an orange)
14 oz (398 mL)	can tomato purée
2 cups (500 mL)	chicken stock
1 ½ cups (375 mL)	dry white wine

½ tsp (2 mL)	salt
½ tsp (2 mL)	ground black pepper
1 lb (500 g)	white potatoes, peeled and cubed

1. Grind the saffron in a mortar and pestle or a spice grinder until it is very fine. Add a few tablespoons (around 30 mL) of hot water to dissolve/dilute it. Set aside.
2. Season the chicken with the rosemary and salt and pepper.
3. Heat the olive oil in a heavy-bottomed pot and brown the chicken in batches, about 5 to 7 minutes, depending on the size of the pieces. Remove the pieces and set aside.
4. Using the same pan, reduce the heat and add the garlic, saffron water, bay leaf, fennel seeds, orange zest, tomato purée, chicken stock, white wine, salt, and pepper.
5. Simmer the mixture for 30 minutes. Remove the bay leaf.
6. Blend the soup using an immersion blender, or skip this step and leave the bouillabaisse more rustic.
7. Remove 1 tsp (5 mL) of this sauce and set aside to make the rouille (see below).
8. Add the potatoes, chicken pieces, and enough water to cover. Cover the pot and simmer for 45 minutes, until the potatoes are tender and the chicken is cooked.

Rouille

½ cup (250 mL)	mayonnaise
2	cloves garlic, pressed
1 tsp (5 mL)	bouillabaisse sauce
	squeeze of lemon juice
	pinch of paprika

Mix ingredients together and put a dollop on top of bouillabaisse, or spread a bit of rouille on a toasted baguette and dip it in the soup.

What to Drink

We've tried this dish with every wine under the sun—yeah, life is tough—but the one style of vino that keeps shining, glass after glass, is a super-chilled, aromatic white. Moillard's "Hugues le Juste" Viognier is good (page 59), Mandrarossa's Fiano is better (page 58), and Loimer's Grüner Veltliner is better still (page 79).

Hand-Me-Down Chicken Vindaloo: Always Better the Next Generation

prep time 45 minutes (20 if using instant paste) | **cooking time** 45 minutes | **serves** 6

If you're ever in Penticton, B.C., and in need of a good used book—or just a great place to hang out for an afternoon—may we suggest The Book Shop. You'll probably run into Bruce, proprietor and notorious cinephile. You might run into his son, Tavis, provided he's not busy collecting vinyl, building a theremin, or making vindaloo. This recipe, given to Bruce by a regular customer, was passed from father to son, and, as most bequeathed recipes go, liberal tweaking of ingredients and methods ensued. In Tavis's words, "It's a mutt of a curry." Enjoy. (Instead of making the vindaloo paste from scratch, you can use a store-bought one such as Patak's—but increase the amount to 3 Tbsp/45 mL for proper heat.)

Vindaloo Paste

¼ cup (60 mL)	ground cumin
3 Tbsp (45 mL)	ground turmeric
2 Tbsp (30 mL)	cayenne pepper
2 Tbsp (30 mL)	ground coriander
1 Tbsp (15 mL)	fenugreek seeds
1 Tbsp (15 mL)	hot mustard powder
2 Tbsp (30 mL)	brown sugar
2 Tbsp (30 mL)	salt
2 Tbsp (30 mL)	ground black pepper
2 tsp (10 mL)	ground ginger
1 tsp (5 mL)	dried chili peppers
1 tsp (5 mL)	ground cinnamon

¾ cup (185 mL)	apple cider vinegar
½ cup (125 mL)	ghee (clarified butter)

1 Combine all the dry ingredients in a bowl.

2 Add the vinegar and mix until a paste is formed. Heat ghee in a saucepan over medium heat.

3 Add the spice mix, reduce heat to low, and cook for 10 minutes, stirring continuously. Set aside.

Chicken Vindaloo

2 lb (1 kg)	skinless, deboned chicken thighs
3 Tbsp	vegetable oil or ghee
2	medium-sized onions, chopped
1	head garlic, peeled and finely chopped
1-inch (2.5 cm)	knob of ginger, finely chopped
2 Tbsp (30 mL)	vindaloo paste (i.e., 1 Tbsp/15 mL per 1 lb/500 g of meat)
½ tsp (2 mL)	salt
14 oz (398 mL)	can diced tomatoes
1 cup (250 mL)	cream
½ cup (125 mL)	water

1 Cut the chicken thighs into pieces. Season with salt and pepper.

2 Heat the vegetable oil in a saucepan on medium heat. Cook the chicken until browned. Remove from the pan and set aside.

3 Using the same pan, heat more oil. Sauté the onions until brown.

4 Add the garlic, ginger, vindaloo paste, and salt. Cook for a minute, mixing well. Reduce heat. Add diced tomatoes and simmer until oil separates.

5 Add the cream and water and simmer for another 10 minutes

6 Purée using an immersion blender, or skip this step if you like a heavier consistency.

7 Add the chicken and simmer for 10 minutes more.

8 Serve on rice or with chapattis, with chilled green grapes on the side.

What to Drink

Donning our lab coats, the fermented key to quenching capsicum heat is not ice-cold white wine. And it's not ice-cold beer, either. It's red wine! With its tannins, a red contains some ten times the concentration of proteins as a white, and as these proteins bind with the capsicum, the flames are doused. Milk does the same thing, but wine is more fun. Rémy Pannier's Chinon (page 120) would put out the fire; likewise, Masi's "Serego Alighieri" (page 128). If it's not working, drink more! It's all in the name of science.

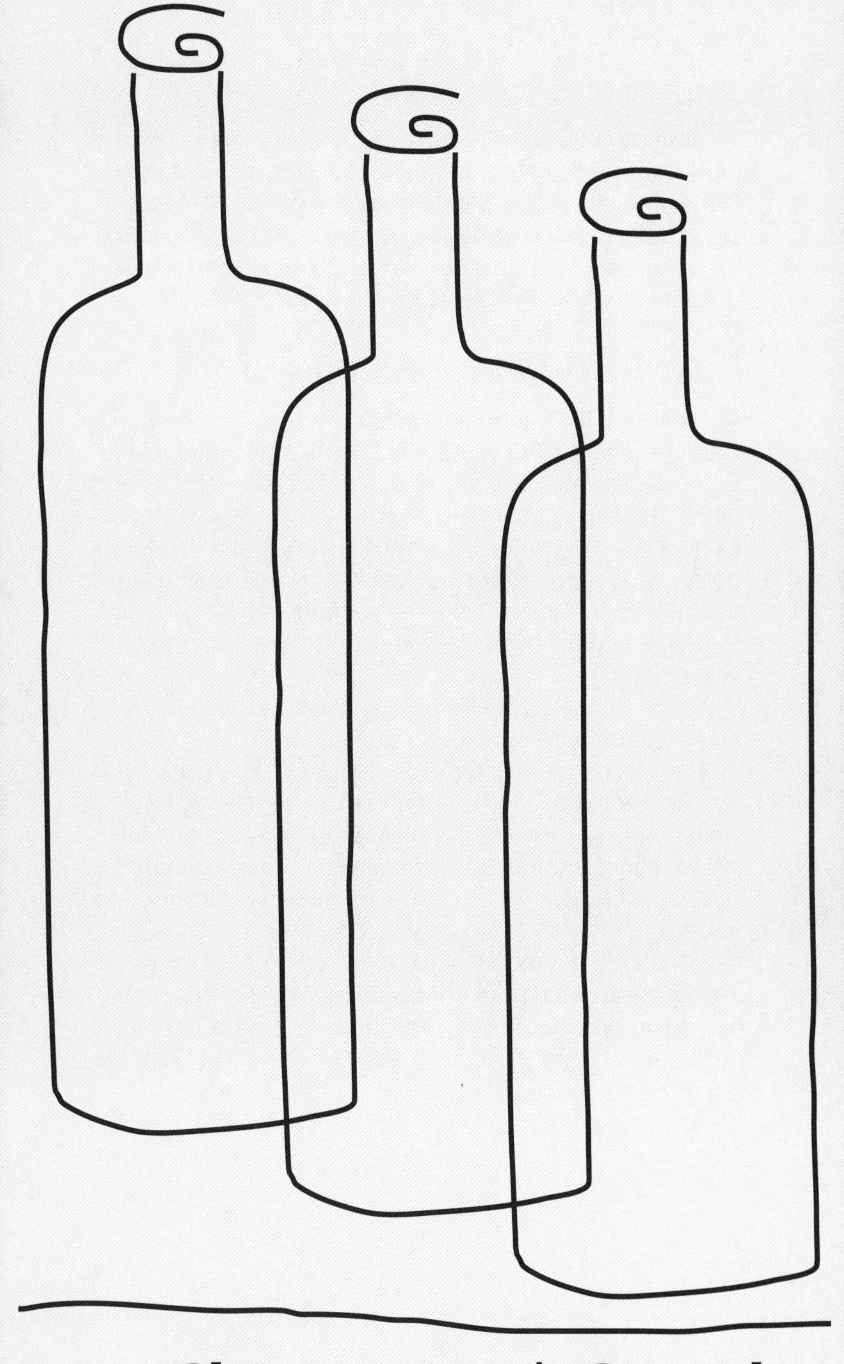

Charts and Graphs

Because we all like to geek out once in a while, here are a handful of charts and graphs derived from our *Had a Glass* tastings. Some of them are based on numbers from this 2010 edition, but in other cases we've taken a five-year look back to see how the wine world has changed. We hope you'll love studying these, especially with a glass of wine in your hand.

France Makes a Lot of Wine: Some of It Is Good

The beauty of this bar chart is twofold. First, we get to see what country wins in 2010. And that's France. It gets the gold for the largest number of delicious wines. Of course, they export one of the largest quantities of wine to the rest of the drinking world, so we're not too surprised. Italy is neck-and-neck export-wise, so the *HAG* stats here kind of make sense. What doesn't jive is Canada! How the heck did so many Canuck wines get into the book? We can only surmise that they must be good.

OK, so domestic availability is skewed in favour of the home team. But drinking local tastes good.

The second great thing about looking at this bar chart is that we get to see which countries excel in reds, are weak in whites, and vice versa. Talking about Canada again, it looks like we harbour some pretty good white wines. Contrast this statistic to Chile and South Africa, where reds clearly rock the house—in the under-$30 category, of course.

What's the take-home? If you're forced to choose between a white versus a red from a given country, bust out this graph, extrapolate your probability, and 88 percent of the time you'll get a winner (with a margin of error of +/– 4.4, i.e., 19 times out of 20).

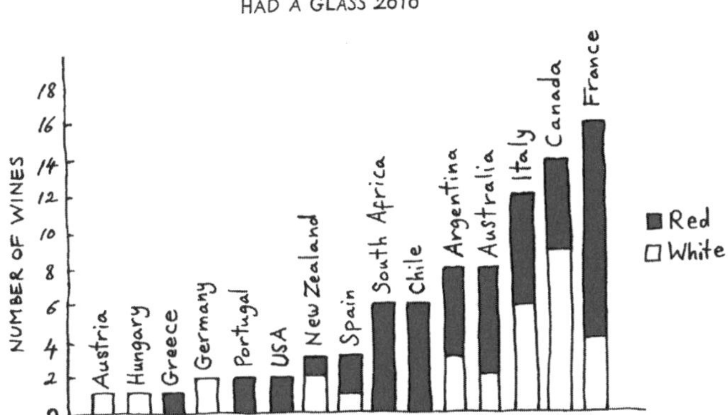

Spreading Value

We assume you noticed that the price point for the 2010 edition got stretched to $30? To show you how this new continuum shakes out in numbers, we have a breakdown of 100 wines by their bottle price.

The take-home? Clearly, despite the extra $10 leeway this year, the bulk of our picks are still in the under-$20 league. What can we say? Value's alive and well and rocking in a price range that we love. The hot spots seem to be $13 and $20.

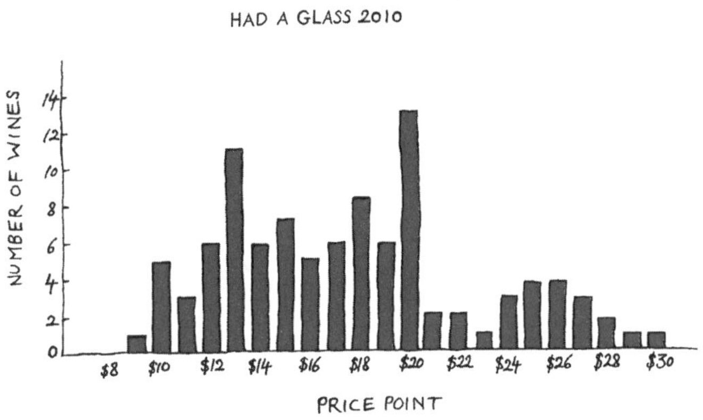

Closure Pie

Screw caps might not be ruling the world yet, but they've sure made strides in the last five years (witnessed at least from *our* tastings). At the same time that cork is losing some footing in the closure market, plastic—or "synthetic" if you like the trade term—is taking a beating. This is just fine by us, because we're not big fans of the neoprene. Sure, it solves the cork taint issue, but it's no good for ageing wine—not to mention that a plastic plug is just déclassé! And we're all about class.

The take-home? Corks are still classic; we're just wary of the one bottle in 20 that's tainted. Realistically, don't sweat the closure too much, but if you've got only one chance and only one bottle of wine, make it a screw cap.

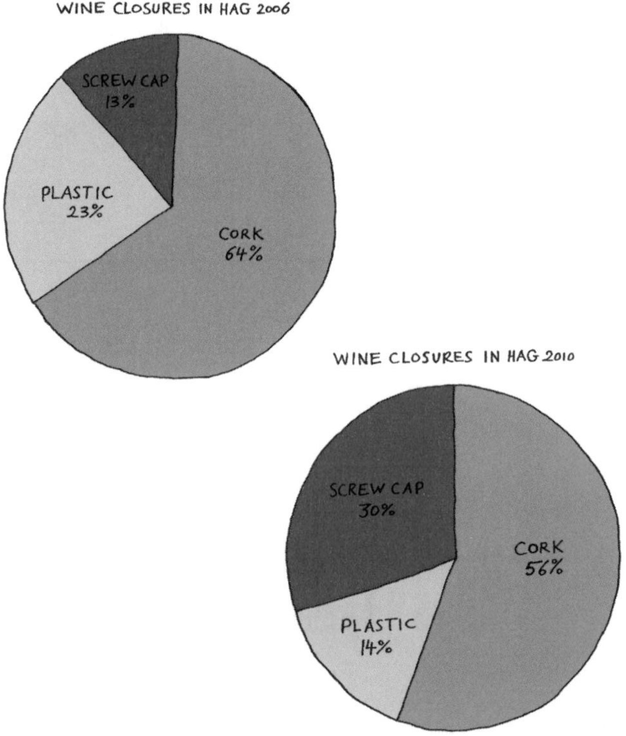

Five-Year Recap

For the fifth anniversary edition of *Had a Glass*, we looked back over the last five years at both the red/white wine split and the Old World/New World split. On reds versus whites, it's interesting to see that the reds are creeping to more numerical significance, although over the past five years we've tasted more and more exciting white wines. So, white wines are standing up and delivering great taste, but just not in numbers.

The Old/New split is pretty much as down the middle as you can get. We didn't plan it this way. Seriously. It's crazy how things shake out.

What's the take-home? We're seeing better and better value from red wines, but, rouge or blanc, whether you shop Europe or the rest of the world, global quality is solid.

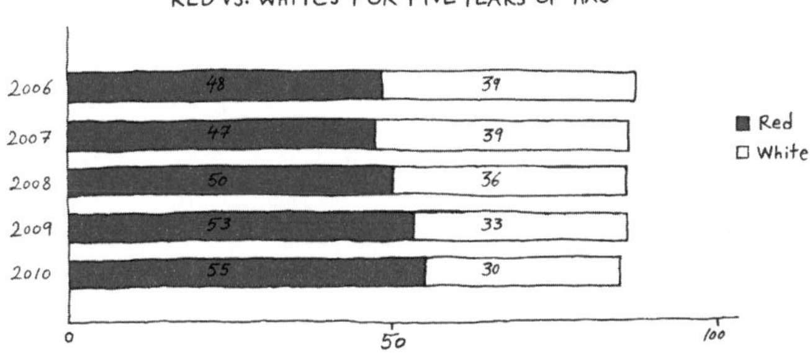

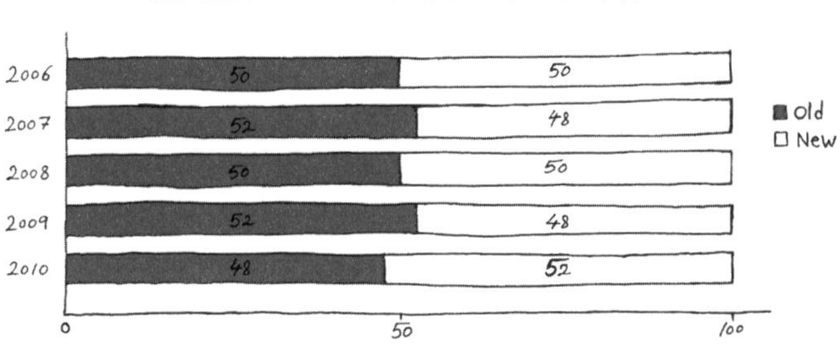

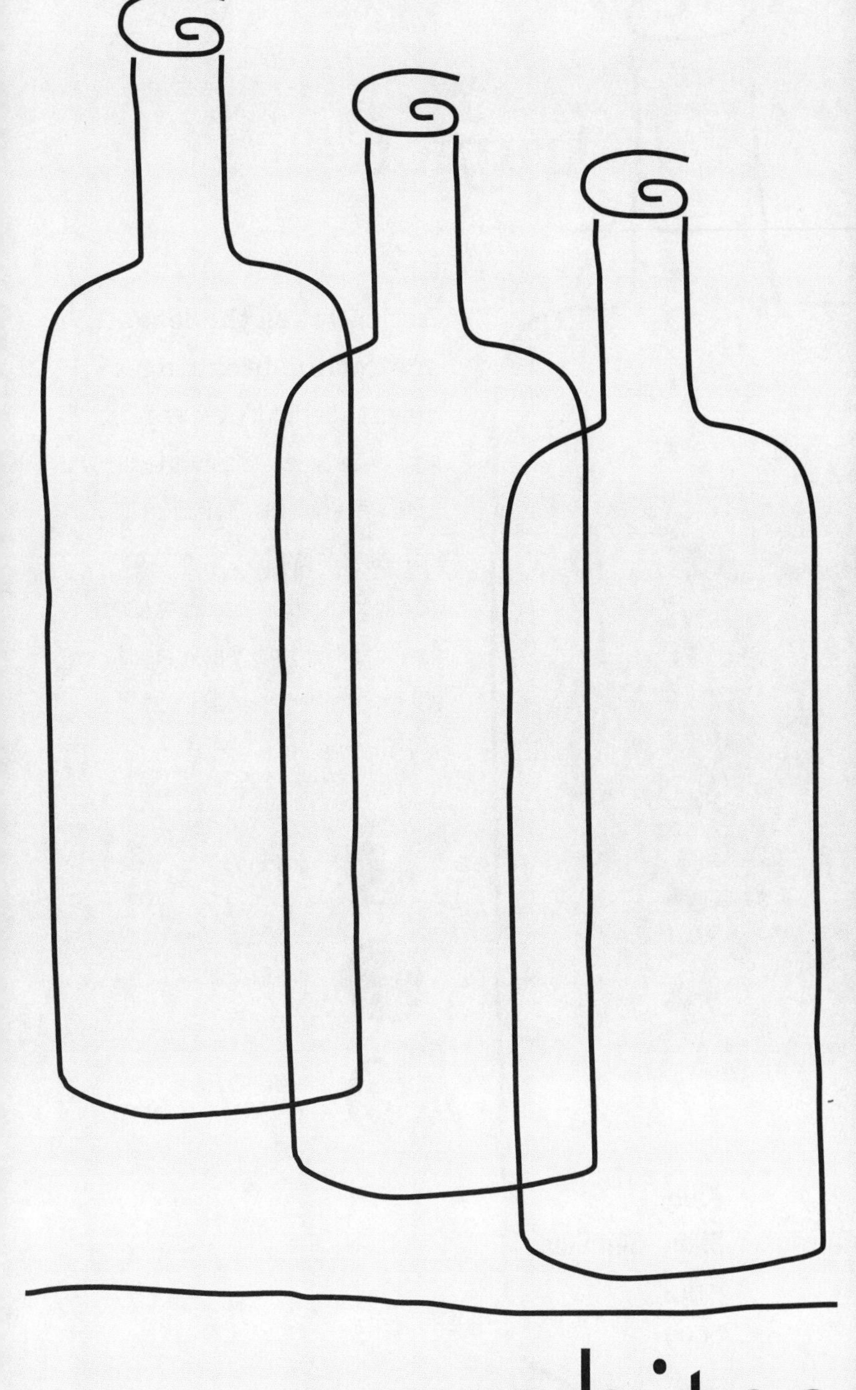

the whites

trapiche

2008
Sauvignon Blanc–Sémillon
"Astica"
$8.99

Astica takes the leadoff spot, while breaking a sweat. That is, if it's been hanging out in the ice bucket like it should be, the bottle will be sweating. But leading off the lineup is no easy task. You gotta get the rally going and set things up to score. Have no fear! This lemony-fresh, smoothly rich, ten-buck brawler knocks it out of the value wine park.

duck curry

masala dosa

Wednesday wine, BYO

Hungary | < $20

dunavar

Every year we suck it up. We hit the streets, twist some caps, and find 100 wines of amazing value. Every wine is unique. We rarely repeat wines from year to year. The wine world is constantly changing, so there are always new and wonderful bottles to choose from. Except for one. The peach aroma, fresh apple, nicely balanced Dunavar has been in our book four out of five years running! It got elbowed out briefly in '09 but it's back and on fire in 2010. We always think, one of these years it's got to go away. But not yet. Oh no.

on its own

beginner

2007
Pinot Gris
$9.49

< $20 | Argentina 

inca

2007
Torrontés-Chardonnay
$10.99

We never get tired of listening to mashups.

From the first time we heard a Rush lick thrown against some booty-shaking bass to whatever Jay-Z vocals get laid over the latest rock track, we dig it. Grapes are harder to mash up. There are great wine blends, but tossing together Torrontés and Chardonnay? This is like power-mixing Petula Clark and Lady Gaga with your ACID Pro. But give it a swirl! You'll get rich nostalgia from the Chard and exotic bouquets from the Torrontés. Quirky, but it sings in the glass, and at a price we can xenochrony out to.

 chicken cordon bleu

 salad rolls

 rock out, BYO

British Columbia | < $20

prospect winery

Thirteen dollars for a shot-in-the-arm Riesling? We're on this wine like white on rice. Like a hungry kid on a Smartie. Like a social media slave on Facebook. Why can't all wine be like this? Plenty of flavour at a workable price. Balance that makes you want to pour the next glass. Versatility that makes you want to pair it up with meals any day of the week. This Riesling's a "gimme."

take-out curry

clam bake

Wednesday wine

2007
Riesling
$12.99

mandrarossa

2007
Fiano
$12.99

Want a curious grape fact? Fiano derives from the Latin *Vitis apiana*, which translates to "vine beloved of bees." Seems our buzzing friends are particularly attracted to this sweet, early-ripening grape. As picturesque as this sounds, we wouldn't want to be in the vineyard—we'd rather be drinking the wine. You'll be quite attracted to the layers of flavour in this budget-conscious white. A great—excuse us—honey, apple, and citrus nose melded with mouth-filling tropical fruits and a simple but fresh finish.

chicken alfredo

scallops

romance, wine geek

France | < $20

moillard

No one can frown while swirling this Viognier.

It teases the tongue with ripe nectarine and floral tones and tickles the nose hairs with a full-on burst of cherry blossoms in spring. Frankly, we get weirded out when we're in a room full of serious sippers; people with their noses deep in the glass and apparently, from the lack of joyous expression, bottles up their butts. There's nothing wrong with smiling when you drink wine. Really. It's OK to show that you're having a good time.

grilled whole trout

on its own

rock out, BYO

2007
Viognier
"Hugues le Juste"
$12.99

< $20 | British Columbia 

peller estates

The damning handle "poor man's Chardonnay" can attach itself to any innocent grape variety, relegating it to public disregard, slander, and general pooh-pooh. Chenin Blanc was once the poor man's Chardonnay. So was Pinot Blanc. Merlot was once Chardonnay's whipping post. Thankfully these varieties have brushed off the discriminations against them and are now making fine wines in their own right—like Peller's primo PB.

Korean stir-fried noodles, aka *jap chae*

Wednesday wine

2008
Pinot Blanc
$12.99

Italy | < $20

primo amore

We're not so sure about the label design, but we'd like to congratulate whoever designed the contents. High five! Hearty bear hug! Secret Masonic handshake! Jive slap! Anyway, as much as Primo Amore is about first love, a reference we don't really get, it's more about straight-up fresh and tasty vino. Chill this as cold as you dare and serve it in your finest plastic cups on the patio. Make a wine slushy, if you dare.

pot stickers

risotto with pesto

aperitif, patio/picnic

2007
Pinot Grigio
$12.99

gehringer brothers

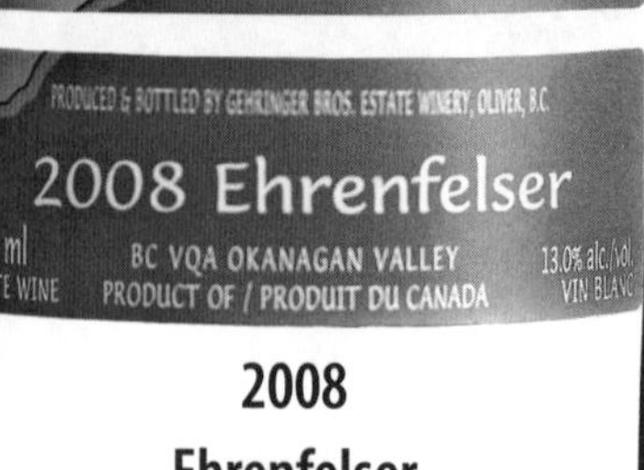

2008 Ehrenfelser "Classic" $13.99

Ehrenfelser is to the patio what Eric B is to Rakim. Each needs the other like a form-fitting drumbeat punctuated by spasmodic scratches needs an eloquent lyricist to drop impeccable locution (rarely evidenced since gangsta glory days). But enough lamenting the loss of old school. It's all about going back to the basics. And nothing is more basically refreshing than a bottle of this Ehrenfelser, chilled to frosty perfection, sipped out of tumblers on the back deck, a boombox blaring away.

on its own

BYO, patio/picnic

Australia | < $20

1st fleet

While Bordeaux may lay historical claim to the Sém–Sauv blend, these days it's the Aussies best embracing (and promoting) the mix's charm. The Sémillon–Sauvignon Blanc combo has become a quintessential Australian white. And why not? It's a style of wine that works as a patio star in the heights of summer or as a pick-me-up in the doldrums of winter. Unctuous, waxy Sémillon gives backbone to the zippy, browbeating citrus-and-canned-pineapple of Sauvignon Blanc. But best of all, the lingering intensity carries through to the finish.

broiled black cod

clam chowder

winter warmer, beginner

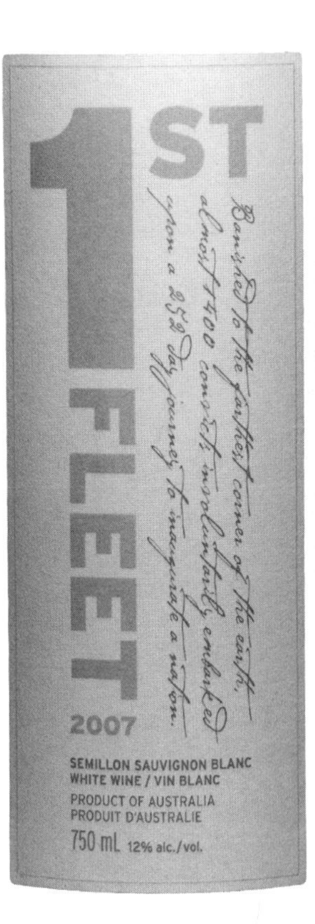

2007
Sémillon–Sauvignon Blanc
$14.99

< $20 | Italy 

araldica

2007
Cortese
$14.99

Wine perfection, in the Had a Glass sense of the word? It doesn't come easy and it doesn't come often. To define perfection: 1) It's two in the afternoon, and we're sitting poolside, sipping wine in Piedmont. 2) We're eating at a restaurant in Piedmont during truffle season and there's lots of Barolo on the menu. 3) Though we're 8,500 kilometres from its home, we can still quaff this fresh, aromatic, and peachy Piedmontese Cortese. This delicious at this price? You could drink it by the bucketful.

on its own

Thai salad

aperitif

 British Columbia | < $20

mt. boucherie

Do you wonder why more Sémillon isn't planted in the Okanagan? We do. It keeps us up at night. If Mt. Boucherie's breathtaking rendition of this Bordeaux variety is any indication of the power of Sémillon, then we're cheering for more. Apple flavours mix with characteristic waxy notes, like you're biting into a Spartan and then smelling a crayon. Believe you us, wine enjoyment doesn't get much better than this.

carrot salad

chicken wings

Wednesday wine

2007
Sémillon
"Estate Collection"
$15.99

voga

Presenting a bottle with its own wine-glass—thereby solving the dilemma of remembering to pack one along with the picnic! This Voga handily comes with a screw-off top that's good for a four-ounce pour. Now if they'd only lose the cork for a screw cap atop the designer bottle as well, we could enjoy the fantastic apple skin, pear, and marzipan flavours of this refreshing Grigio all the more, without wasting the brain cells it takes to remember to bring along a corkscrew.

VOGA ITALIA
PINOT GRIGIO

2007
Pinot Grigio
$15.99

bánh mì

pasta primavera

patio/picnic,
Wednesday wine

France | < $20

dourthe

The best Bordeaux in this book is: 1) $17, 2) an easy rival for anything twice the price, and 3) a white wine. With exactly zero percent of anything Cabernet or Merlot in this bottle, one wonders where the white Bordeaux have been hiding all this time. Forget the snazzy Sauvignons of the world. Go back to the source to see how it can get done up right: guava and gooseberry in a stunning, palate-caressing, fresh-out-of-the-gate, crispy white wine.

baked oysters

romance

2007
Bordeaux
"Dourthe No. 1"
$16.99

wirra wirra

2007
Sauvignon Blanc/
Sémillon/Viognier
"Scrubby Rise"
$16.99

This blend's got punch.

Wirra Wirra takes the classic Aussie white grape partners of Sauvignon Blanc and Sémillon and then turns things up a notch with a rich kiss of Viognier. The wine that comes out of the blender is an impossibly delicious compendium that highlights all three varietals. We're talking fresh grass, lanolin and herbs, a whiff of apricot pit and lees, and a fresh citrus finish—fantastic complexity with elegant balance.

 on its own

 tofu stir-fry

 rock out, BYO

cedarcreek

In the big, bad world of wine, grapes can taste different depending on their genesis. And then there is Riesling. Riesling is the single most diverse drink we can think of (and that's after a lot of real thinking). It can be minerally and mouth-puckering, like you're sucking on rocks and lemons, or so delicate and saccharine that you want to go to bed with it (in a platonic way, of course), or it can be like CedarCreek's genius rendition: tropical and as exciting as winning a lottery.

belly

steamed mussels

Wednesday wine

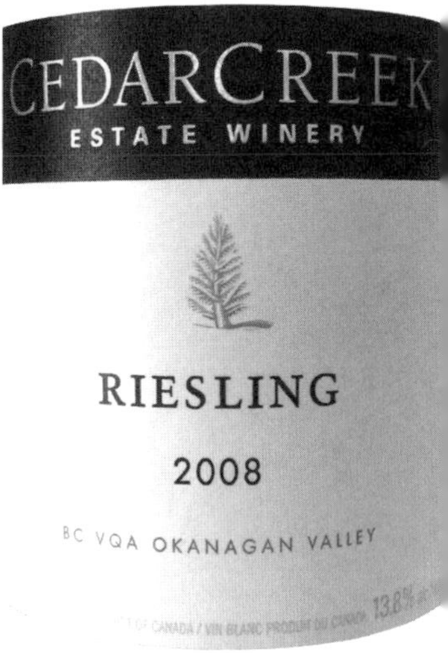

2008
Riesling
$17.90

< $20 | Germany

bex

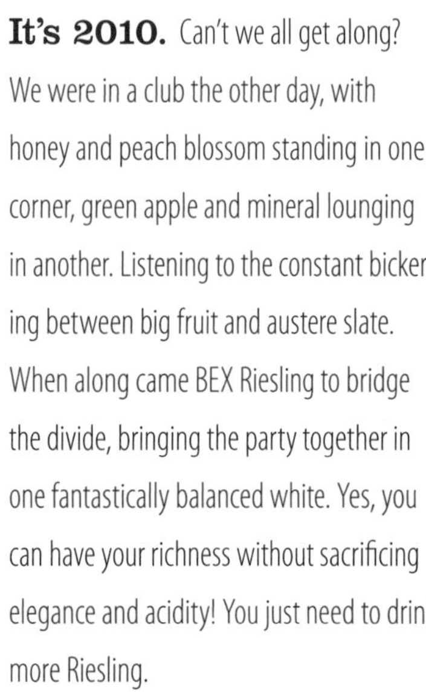

It's 2010. Can't we all get along? We were in a club the other day, with honey and peach blossom standing in one corner, green apple and mineral lounging in another. Listening to the constant bickering between big fruit and austere slate. When along came BEX Riesling to bridge the divide, bringing the party together in one fantastically balanced white. Yes, you can have your richness without sacrificing elegance and acidity! You just need to drink more Riesling.

2006
Riesling
$17.99

honey-glazed ham

Morbier

cellar, wine geek

Spain | < $20

parés baltà

Meet the Parés Hilton of the wine world! This flamboyant and fresh, paparazzi-pleasing Blanc de Pacs will not be happy until it's served at every exclusive party. Or at least on top of every patio table. Classic Cava grapes keep it "still" in this fantastic bottle. We're talking Parellada, Xarel-lo, and Macabeo: the stars of Spanish sparkling wine—fermented dry, without the fizz. The result is just as thirst-quenching and lemony-limey, with a remarkable balance. This flashy white will have everyone talking.

bacon-wrapped asparagus

seared scallops

patio/picnic,
rock out

2007
Blanc de Pacs
$17.99

 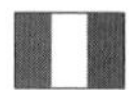

bollini

Time to take back Grigio! The rest of the wine world needs to get up off of Italy's wine press and stick to the Gris moniker. We're tired of poseur Grigios jumping on the wine fashion bandwagon and taking up good space in our glasses. Skip all that and grab a bottle of Bollini for the real deal. This Trentino treasure tantalizes with aromas of fresh-picked flowers, citrus, and apple skin, followed by fantastic intensity. Fresh and balanced, just like a fine Italiano Grigio. Cin cin.

2007
Pinot Grigio
$18.99

spicy salt squid

ginger chicken

patio/picnic, beginner

Ontario | < $20

cave spring

West Coasters don't get to taste a lot of wines from the East. It's as if there's a wine wall that runs north–south somewhere between the Pacific and Eastern time zones, possibly in Saskatchewan. Attempts are occasionally made to get an Ontario wine listed in B.C. and vice versa, but the risk of getting caught, and the punitive sentence of lethal oxidization, deters many. One of the successful crossings is Cave Spring's Riesling, from the Niagara Peninsula—a wine of courage and fortitude, with tenacious aromas of petrol, mineral, apple, and lime rind.

bratwurst, sauerkraut, potatoes

wine geek, romance

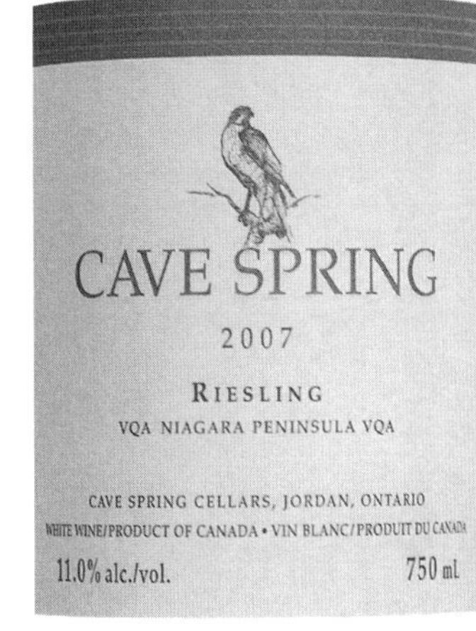

2007
Riesling
$18.99

< $20 | Argentina 

crios

2008
Torrontés
$18.99

Who would've thought having your mouth washed out with soap could be so tasty? The Crios Torrontés is impossibly floral and full of aromatic potpourri. It's like smelling and drinking a bar of soap—in the best possible way! Perhaps we should have been mouthier as kids; instead we had to wait until legal age to experience such a taste. This is one assertive, fresh, fun, and original white.

 on its own

 sweet and sour cod

 patio/picnic, rock out

Germany | < $20

loosen bros.

A three-bottle night can end in one of two ways. Very badly. Or very, very well. As in, you're still licking your lips savouring the slate and lime-rind finish of a so-easy-quaffing-it-should-be-a-crime German Riesling. With ABVs reaching for the stratosphere these days, at the point in the night when you are removing the cork from that third bottle of wine, we can say from experience you are likely walking down a road to certain demise. But! For those thirsty times, Dr. L comes to the rescue to promote moderation and continued good times with its characteristic 8.5 percent alcohol and fine flavour.

on its own

risotto

BYO, winter warmer

DR LOOSEN BROS
2007
Riesling

2007
Mosel
Riesling
"Dr. L"
$18.99

wild goose

What's in a vintage? For most large-scale wine productions, where we're talking hundreds of thousands of bottles (or bags in boxes) a year, we find that a particular vintage is less of an influence than the blending of wines that created a particular style. Not that there's anything wrong with that. Some of these mega-winery wines are in these pages, but only if they're good. When discussing smaller, family-run, hands-on operations, then vintage can be a quality marker. Or de-marker. 2008 in the Okanagan was a gracious boon for white wines, particularly aromatic white wines, and Wild Goose's "Gew" is a mouth-watering example.

2008
Gewürztraminer
$18.99

butternut squash soup

romance

France | < $20

château de chasseloir

Fresh is all about context.

"Don't get fresh with me," she railed.

"She's FRESH," sang Kool & the Gang.

"Fresh, exciting."

"Feeling fresh as a daisy," he exhaled after his nap.

"That's fresh," the urbanite, circa 1990, extolled, drawing his buddy's attention to the latest "it" thing.

"This is a fresh wine," the wine writers opined, as they cracked open a bottle of Chasseloir Muscadet.

mussels with any sauce

grilled chicken

patio/picnic, Wednesday wine

2007
Muscadet Sèvre et Maine Sur Lie
$19.95

chartron & trebuchet

Burgundy on a budget doesn't get much better than this. As soon as you read the label and see that classy word "Bourgogne," you already know you're digging for $25, $26—maybe $27. So, while this is no "Poo-lig-knee" (Pouligny) or "Sha-sang" (Chassagne), it is a $20 intro to the leesy, melon, and pear delight that we love about "Boar-gone," brought to you by a stand-up *négociant* and packaged with a classy label.

2007
Bourgogne
Chardonnay
$19.99

clam linguini

Époisse

romance

Austria | < $20

loimer

Something about drinking Grüner just makes you want to rock. Toss something on the stereo (the fewer chords the better), crank the volume knob past ten, and pour the glass to the brim. Grüner Veltliner is a rock star grape. It strums a natural crispness and minerality with a beguiling richness. Not only does the Loimer have a rockin' neon green label, it struts out showing wet stone, tangy pomelo, and spicy white pepper powder before powering a rich finish home.

char sui

raclette

wine geek, rock out

2007
Grüner Veltliner
"Lois"
$19.99

township 7

When we taste wines for *Had a Glass*, we don't always just randomly try a bottle here and a bottle there. We often pull up our chairs and get to work on a flight, at least three related bottles at one time. So, if we taste Cabernets, then we try X, Y, and Z Cabernets. When we sat down for this wine, we had it flanked by a Township 6 and a Township 8. Numero 7 was the hands-down winner: tropical fruits complemented by fig and toasty oak. It leans to the rich side of the Chard spectrum, with a nice baking-spice finish to comfort the palate.

2007 Chardonnay $19.99

 tandoori chicken

 Cincinnati chili

 winter warmer

New Zealand | < $25

longbush

There are two types of Gewürztraminers in this world: First, the kind that is all peachy, flowery, and zippy on the tongue. What is commonly referred to as a "patio sipper." The deck chug-a-lugger. The balcony guzzler. Then there is the kind of Gewürztraminer that you don't sip. It sips you instead. We're talking about mean street oiliness, bulldozer lychee, and browbeating honey effects. You don't see a wine like this very often, but when you do, get it. Or it will get you.

on its own

brie

aperitif

2007
Gewürztraminer
$20.99

tantalus

The sun was still high when we began to get thirsty. We opened the fridge door and inside were a great number of bottles. We opened one and poured its contents into our glasses. We drank it, but our thirst persisted. We returned to the fridge and took out a different bottle. We took long and deliberate sips, and the bottle was soon empty. And we were still thirsty. We opened a Tantalus Riesling next. The clean mineral and lime flavours raced down our gullets, and the bracing acidity scratched at our taste buds. The wine was good, and we felt relief.

2008
Riesling
$22.90

 salad with good ricotta

 choucroute garnie

 cellar

Italy | < $25

principessa gavia

Salute the rebirth of subtle! With wines getting more and more profuse in the last decade (more oak! more extraction! more alcohol! more everything!), we're on the cusp of big-wine backlash. Wine drinkers are getting tired. Our palates have been overstimulated for so many vintages that we need a break. Not a break from wine, of course, but to enjoy a bottle of Principessa. This stony, apple, and citrus measure of taste tranquility is the type of wine that's going to be the next big thing.

oysters on a half shell

Caesar salad

patio/picnic

2007
Gavi
$23.99

staete landt

We don't typically buy $30 wines. So it's fair to say that at this price point we want wine that's unafraid to strut its stuff. In this more rarefied air, value wines are those bottles that aren't just made for happy quaffing. They unabashedly speak of the land they're from. We don't just want a Sauvignon Blanc; we demand a "Marlborough" Sauvignon Blanc and all the tropical-fruit-meets-fresh-cut-grass-zippiness-melded-with-beguiling-minerality-and-fantastical-depth that comes with the true territory. We want Staete Landt.

2007
Sauvignon Blanc
"Marlborough"
$27.99

 fondue

 chicken strips

 romance, winter warmer

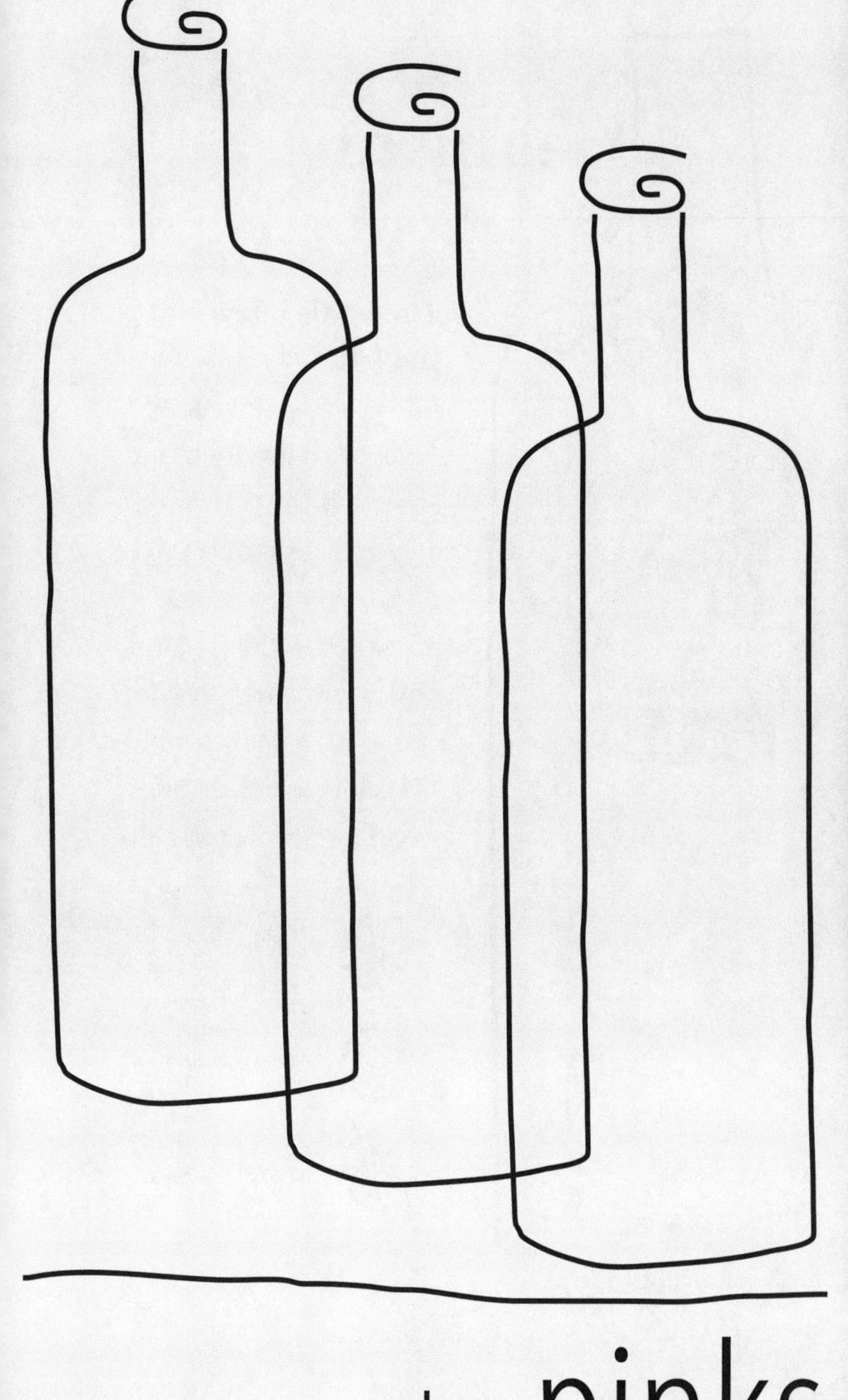

the pinks

jeanjean

The bottle curves to the left. What more needs to be said? Conservative wine drinkers will no doubt steer clear of this left-leaning, pinky wine. But that's their issue—all the more lush-cherry-fruit, easy-sipping vino for us. At this price, the whole populace could be drinking pink. Wine socialism! Serve this bottle nice and chilled on the patio, and we guarantee you won't have any complaints (though you may start a rosé revolution).

on its own

Peking duck pizza

patio/picnic, romance

2007
Syrah Rosé
$11.99

Chile | < $20

miguel torres

We love the classic rosé. But when we tasted this electric-blush-coloured Chilean pink, we weren't about to go Luddite. Tons of rhubarb and cherry-pie aromas ooze out of the glass before some rich, sweet cherry goes tête-à-tête with a tart, ruby-red-grapefruit finish. This is a fun, vivacious, modern pink wine, more like rosé on 'roids.

spicy riblets

nachos

winter warmer, wine geek

2008
Cabernet Sauvignon Rosé
"Santa Digna"
$13.99

< $20 | Spain 

marqués de cáceres

2008
Rioja Rosado
$16.49

A checklist for the top three spots to drink rosé:

- ☐ Rooftop hotel bar, poolside. Check.
- ☐ Out in the woods, with an ice bucket and an iPod hookup. Check.
- ☐ On a cliff at sunset, waves crashing below, lost somewhere along the Mediterranean. Check.

The classy, and classic, Cáceres Rosado comes through at all of the above.

ceviche

tenderloin with mole sauce

patio/picnic, Wednesday wine

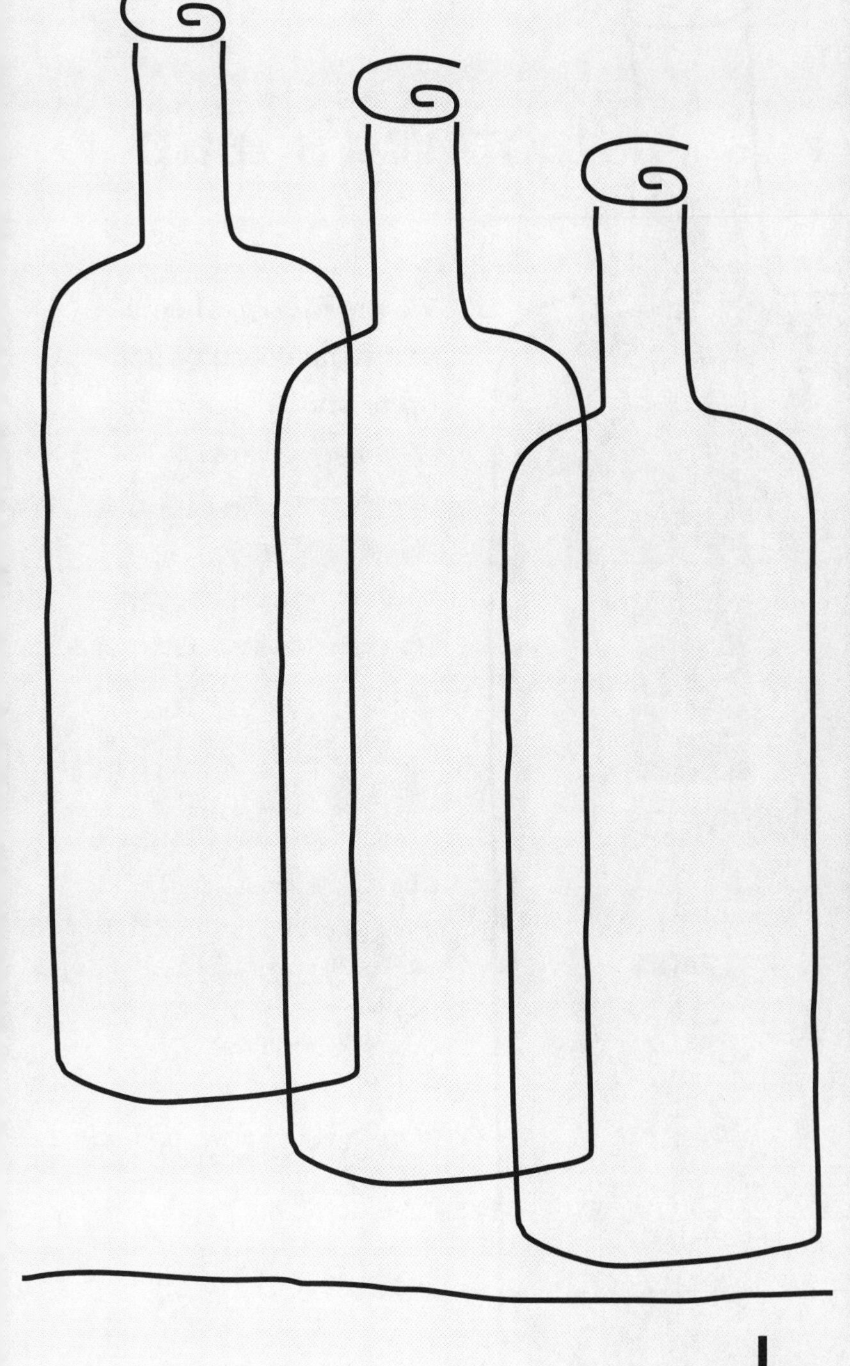

the reds

< $20 | South Africa 

leopard's leap

We get angry when a $12 wine doesn't taste up to snuff. When this happens, our friends shake their heads. "It's $12. Of course it's going to taste like this," they say, having long ago resigned themselves to mediocre expectations. We refuse to forsake quality, no matter the cheapness. There *is* good $12 wine out there. Wine that doesn't taste like rubber bands or weasel piss, and there could be—should be—more. Like the Lookout, an easy-going wine with flavours of ripe plum and raspberry.

on its own

pan-fried sirloin

beginner

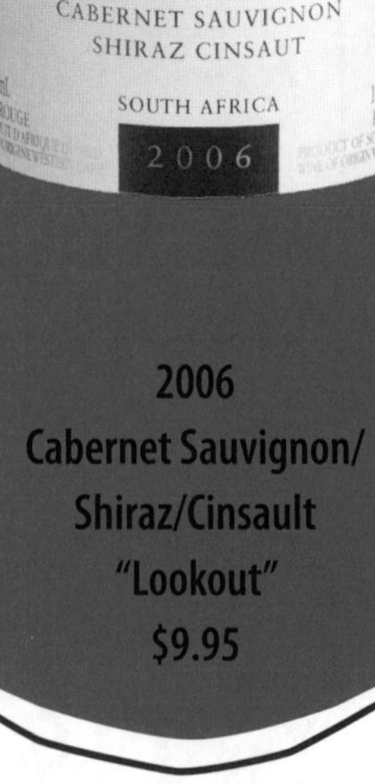

2006
Cabernet Sauvignon/
Shiraz/Cinsault
"Lookout"
$9.95

South Africa | < $20

obikwa

Value is relative and non-denominational.

Unfortunately, the going rate for "value" seems to have exponentially outpaced inflation. Bear witness to $10M for an 82-game season, or billions for the latest unprofitable "social media" website. But fear not, fellow wine drinker! We found Obikwa—cheap and cheerful—lurking in South Africa among the Shiraz vines. It saunters up to the palate with soft, rich plum, pepper, and smoked-sausage flavours and offers up more easy-drinking flavour than $10 has ever seen before.

burgers

on its own

Wednesday wine, rock out

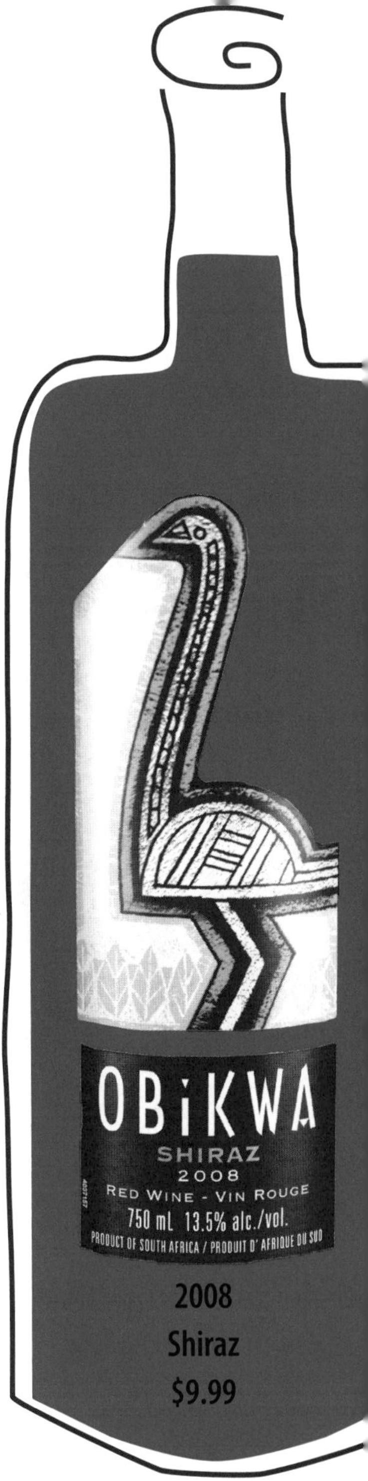

2008
Shiraz
$9.99

terra andina

There are many paths to wine enjoyment. Mid-week, when we've only got a ten spot in the wallet for a wine—and it needs to be both nourishing and potable—we'll walk out with Caminos. Its fruit-forward, ripe, and smooth style pairs up just fine with a diverse array of food, and its easy-peasy sipping style will scream, "drink me up."

lasagna

chili

BYO, winter warmer

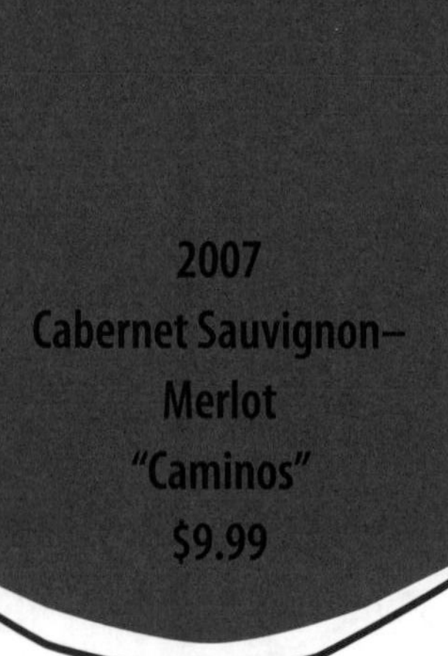

South Africa | < $20

tribal

Follow the wine label golden ratio: For every five wines you buy based on their catchy labels, choose a sixth that's downright ugly. If you only buy pretty, you run the grievous risk of completely missing out on Tribal's Pinotage. It's a scary leap of faith, we know. Both the name and the label on this bottle run counter to most people's "buy me" sensibilities. But buy ugly just this once, and you'll get bang-on quaffing flavour for a tenner.

hot dogs, lots of fixings

Wednesday wine

TRIBAL
PINOTAGE
SOUTH AFRICA

2006
Pinotage
$9.99

finca los primos

We are all over the braise these days. It's magical, really. Take a cheap cut of meat, brown it in a cast-iron pot with some onions and veggies, toss in a generous amount of red wine, and a few hours later you've got mouth-watering, fork-tender, rich protein. The Finca Malbec is total braising wine. Heck, it's so budget friendly you can buy two bottles—one for the meat, and one for the cook.

 braised shank

 braised ribs

 BYO, Wednesday wine

South Africa | < $20

two oceans

The Two Oceans Shiraz is a confluence of savoury and sweet.

Sausage casing and leather come head-to-head with a burst of plush strawberry fruit. And before trying to intellectualize this go-to red any further, lock out your inner wine Einsteins and remember that this is an $11 bottle! Its smooth, easygoing style screams for good times any day of the week. And that's about as close to our *vinous operandi* as it gets.

roast turkey

squid ink pasta

Wednesday wine, BYO

2008
Shiraz
$10.99

< $20 | Argentina 

bodega del fin del mundo

#valuewines. @james — tsted n.e gud value wines 2dy? **@kenji** — nu vntg of sthrnmst red, its kickin: frsh, plmy, chrry **@james** — solid, how $ **@kenji** — stdy at $12 **@james** — coolio **@kenji** — l8tr sk8tr

chimichurri

kebabs

wine geek, Wednesday wine

2008
"Southern Most Red"
$11.99

Spain | < $20

castaño

This Monastrell has mass appeal. The price tag plays well to savvy sippers. The flavour hounds get juiced by its layers of plump plum and raspberry, licorice, herby earth, and a lashing of oak. The artiste hipsters get turned on by both of the above plus the stylish, pseudo-Constructivist, type-heavy label. Sip en masse.

burgers

dark chocolate

rock out, patio/picnic

2006
Monastrell
$11.99

meia encosta

Though a scientist of little renown, Bac Chus developed a set of early-19th-century laws that we still find relevant.

Chus's First Law specifies that grape juice plus yeast equals wine. His Second Law states that the process is common and should not be glamorized. The Third Law, a continuance, says that, with respect to the first two laws, we are all entitled to great table wine that doesn't cost absurd amounts of cash.

Dão
DENOMINAÇÃO DE ORIGEM CONTROLADA
Meia Encosta
VINHO TINTO / RED WINE — 2006
PRODUTO DE PORTUGAL / PRODUCT OF PORTUGAL
SOCIEDADE DOS VINHOS BORGES SA

2006
Dão
$11.99

black bean soup

Wednesday wine

 Italy | < $20

vitae

Writing a résumé sucks. Lining up action verbs with measurable outcomes, incorporating buzzwords, spell-checking. We applied to work for *Wine Spectator*, hoping to impress with a tasting speed of 30 wines per hour, but we didn't get an interview. They were looking for "proven ability to incorporate 15 adjectives into a wine review." We'd written ten. Soft, ripe cherry, crowd pleasing, spicy oak finish, classy retro bottle. At least the Vitae is a workhorse of a wine.

 pepperoni pizza

 Cheddar

 BYO, aperitif

2007
Sangiovese
$12.45

château de valcombe

A good friend, and known wine fiend, tipped us off about this wine. We asked him, "What are you drinking these days?" He said, "That's Easy. Valcombe. I buy it by the case." We bought a bottle too. We cracked it. We loved it. We polished it off and went back for more. We don't think there's any room for debate. Here's a flavourful expression of the down-south of France: a herb, blackberry, and plum delight. Something you can put up your sleeve and turn your friends onto.

miso-marinated steak

coq au vin

BYO

Italy | < $20

masi

This is commuting wine. And no, we're not talking about drinking and driving. The most enjoyable commute is the civilized 25-minute ferry ride from Hong Kong Central to Discovery Bay. We still salivate over the thought as we sit idling in gridlock. OK, so a commute is a commute and still means time tossed to the wind, but get this: before boarding the catamaran, you can stop off at the nautical-themed, hole-in-the-wall Anchor Pub for a "road Coke." We'd pick a glass of Masi's easygoing, bright plum, imminently smooth red Rosso, ideal to melt the day's work away while sipped safely from a seaworthy plastic cup.

mushroom frittata

sweet and sour pork

Wednesday wine

MASI
MODELLO DELLE VENEZIE

2007
Modello delle Venezie
$12.99

terramater

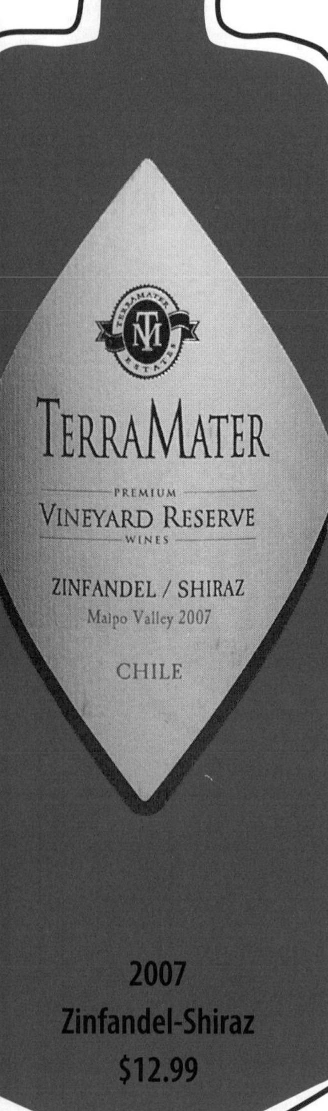

What's with the bromance? Where did all these romantic guy comedy flicks come from? We thought dudes were supposed to be tough and macho, but all of a sudden, before we can shout, "I Love You, Man," there are heartfelt homeboys all over the big screen. Wearing their emotions on their sleeves (albeit with fart jokes and projectile vomiting). Aw well! Pop in the DVD and pour a glass of this quirky Seth Rogen–like Zin-Shiraz blend. Its unfiltered, smooth cinnamon and strawberry jam flavours, backed up by a peppery finish, make it a wine for the times.

caramel corn

meatloaf

romance, beginner

South Africa | < $20

nederburg

There are two Pinotages in HAG 2010. This is a first. We're getting serious about it because it's getting serious about us. Allow us to explain. Pinotage is that weird and wacky variety from South Africa about which we occasionally, yet poetically, wax on. Occasionally being the operative word. But for 2010, we tasted more, and better, Pinotage than ever before. Which we think means the skilled South African vintners are getting into Pinotage with more enthusiasm.

shin, oxtail, or similar stew

mabo tofu

wine geek

2007
Pinotage
$13.00

mcguigan

2007
Shiraz
"Black Label"
$13.50

If a flashy, trendy, animal-adorned label can convince us to pony up sight unseen—or untasted—can a stodgy, orthodox one make us think twice? With its tweed jacket and its shirt tucked in, McGuigan doesn't own the flash style, but pour a glass of this under-the-radar Shiraz and you'll find that wine doesn't have to have a pretty face to taste. Nine out of ten trendsetters agree: the button-down look is in!

jerk or BBQ chicken

beginner, rock out

Portugal | < $20

cortello

Pour this Vinho Tinto for guests and you'll have them thinking you must've brought out the fancy wine. The VIP treatment? Oh yeah! But far from feigning nobility, this lush blend of Castelão and Aragonez (Portuguese for Tempranillo)—all plush and plump with opulent plum, a hint of orange peel, sage, and savoury herbs—is a populist bottle at this price.

Burger King

loin chops

winter warmer, BYO

2006
Vinho Tinto
$13.99

< $20 | France 

moillard

No thugged-out Pinot, this is the OG of the value camp. It'll battle toe-to-toe with any wine out there that claims varietal integrity and affordability. The rest can brush the dirt off their (sloped) shoulders because "Huge the Juice" is in the house. It's hotter than a hot slice and spitting rhymes like a true Pinot Noir, not some poser trying to live large by bumping phony bling. Cherry. Raspberry. And some forest floor that would make Givry jump. This wine is fresh.

prosciutto sandwich

patio/picnic

2007
Pinot Noir
"Hugues le Juste"
$13.99

Chile | < $20

palo alto

We're tired of bad Don Cherry suits and mass-produced lager. Yes, we tempt cries of sacrilege when we go on record to say that beer isn't the only libation of choice to pair with hockey. Look, we'll drink from your sippy cups in the arena, but at home, it's not Miller time. It's time to cheer on the boys with a gutsy red. The Palo Alto is nicely balanced, with ripe blackberry fruit and a smoky, toasty finish. Perfect for the first, second, or third periods. Overtime might need another bottle.

puck-sized tenderloins

Cheezies

winter warmer, rock out

2007
"Reserva"
$14.97

folonari

2007
Valpolicella
$14.99

Are the days of glass bottles numbered? Perhaps, but let's take a moment to thank our hardened sandy friend. If it weren't for glass, we might still be drinking wine from animal skins. Little-known fact: Folonari saved our wine-drinking selves by investing in and pioneering the distribution of wine in glass. So we'll happily salute them with a glass of their mouth-filling, fresh, scintillating, cherry-flavoured Valpolicella. Of course, as we come around to putting a price on greenhouse gases, we'll be happy to pour our Valpo out of a more carbon-friendly Tetra Pak.

salmon

antipasto

aperitif, BYO

France | < $20

les brottiers

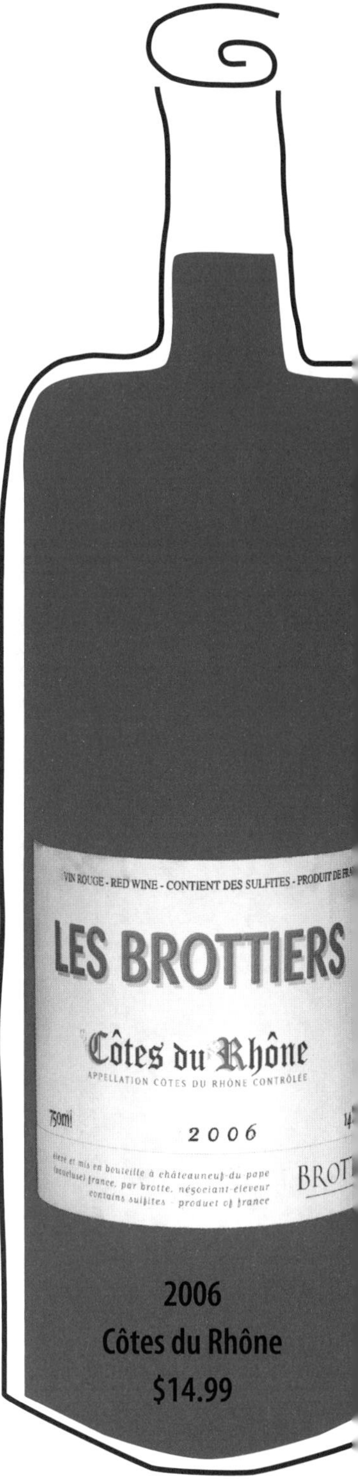

Seduction takes many forms. We polled our friends and found that eight out of ten people get lucky on Grenache. Eight out of ten people think that good Grenache jumps out of the glass and tickles the taste buds with lush berry fruit and a sultry slap of spice. Eight out of ten people found that Les Brottiers did the trick. It didn't hurt that Serge Gainsbourg was crooning away on the stereo on a starry, snowy night in a wood stove–warmed cabin in the woods.

côte de bœuf

roast

winter warmer, BYO

2006
Côtes du Rhône
$14.99

< $20 | France 

louis bernard

What's the deal with Villages? You've got your Côtes du Rhône-Villages and your Beaujolais Villages. Do people in villages make better wine? Why do we care about the oeno-logical prowess of these village people? The quick answer is that "Villages" connotes a more limited geography—areas traditionally known for producing high-quality grapes. In the case of Côtes du Rhône, only 95 communes—or villages—out of the 171 in the AOC have a right to bear the flying V. The LB CdR-V is a Grenache, Syrah, Mourvèdre, and Cinsault blend of super-cracked black pepper intensity, with lots of punchy plum and mellow cocoa aromatics.

pulled pork

winter warmer, rock out

2006
Côtes du Rhône-Villages
$15.99

maison des bulliats

Maybe we're not making ourselves clear.

Cru Beaujolais (like this Régnié) is the wine of the future. We have pontificated on the merits of proper Beaujolais for the past few editions of this book. But you are still not getting on board. We still see bottles on the shelf. Where have you been? What have you been drinking? The play is a four-seamer to quality Beaujolais. We are tired of big, fat, ass-kicking wines. We want wines we can drink with a meal. Wines that, when we look at a bottle, we ask, "Where did that go?"

carrot soup

Morbier

patio/picnic, Wednesday wine

2006
Régnié
$15.99

< $20 | Argentina 

punto final

It seems, from our ivory tower of wine analysis (more like a dingy living room with a load of open bottles, dirty glasses, and scribbled wine notes), that Malbec was once hot. Then it was not. Well, now it's hot again. Why? We don't know. Maybe it was a mad cow thing. But when a gem like this Punto Final busts onto the dilly-dallying scene at $16 and waves around all its berry fruit, leather, and spice, we must conclude Malbec is back.

Salisbury steak

romance

2007
Malbec
$15.99

Australia | < $20

hellbent

Great! June 4th/10

So we rented the movie Hellbent the other night. We popped the popcorn and plopped down on the couch. All of a sudden we're seeing two dudes on dates get popped in the park. And on the night before the West Hollywood Halloween festival! What are Chaz, Joey, Eddie, and Tobey to do?!? Hellbent the wine is just as campy, but thankfully shows much, much better than the flick. Gobs of blackberry and cherry fruit are anything but scary in this fruit-forward, well-structured swirler that is sure to get the party jumping.

kebabs

on its own

rock out, patio/picnic

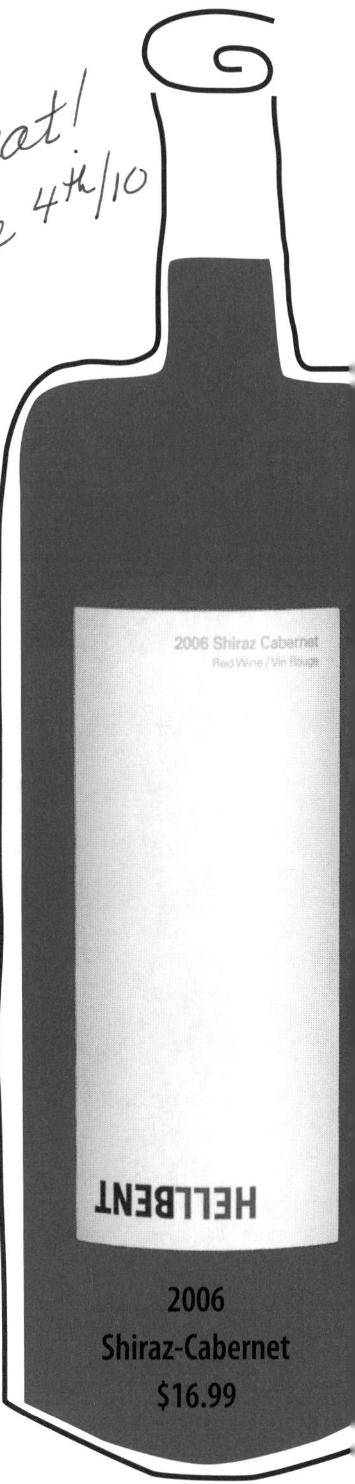

2006 Shiraz Cabernet
Red Wine / Vin Rouge
HELLBENT

2006
Shiraz-Cabernet
$16.99

< $20 | France

Teaming the white grape Viognier up with Syrah seems to be the hottest wine trend since the glass bottle took over from the wineskin. We're talking just a drop of Viognier (in the 1 to 5 percent range) into the red. Not enough to make a pink, but just enough to tweak the aromatic profile. Taking it back to the Old World, wines from the Rhône's Côte Rotie have had this mix for generations, and we bet they're scratching their beards watching the rest of the world go gaga over the concept. Hear! Hear! to Paul Mas for going back to the roots and coming up big with this winning bottle.

2007
Syrah-Viognier
$16.99

chicken cacciatore

winter warmer

California | < $20

matchbook

When the dollar did its brief but enthusiastic climb against the U.S. currency late in 2007, it had us licking our lips for some better pricing on California juice. A couple of bargains surfaced, but it wasn't like we could get any Alexander Valley Cabernet or Santa Barbara Pinot for $10. Our hopes were dashed until we stumbled on this particular wine. Here's some Dunnigan Hills Syrah paired with Chalk Hill Cabernet in an aromatic, spicy blend of juiciness that sings value for under $20.

on its own

grilled chicken

beginner, romance

2006
Syrah–Cabernet Sauvignon
$16.99

ruffino

2006 Chianti "Il Leo" $16.99

We're not quite sure how Ruffino gets real-deal Chianti flavour into a $17 bottle of wine. Maybe 2006 saw a yard sale on Sangiovese in the rolling Tuscan hills, but frankly, we don't care. If all your inexpensive Chianti has only come in a bulbous bottle clothed in wicker wrapping, then we suggest you make haste to your nearest liquor store and buy one—nay, two! three!—bottles of this blindingly delicious value.

Korean short ribs

spaghetti and meatballs

romance

chono

This is the first wine we've tasted from Chile's Elqui Valley.

Taking a long slurp from the glass, we were suddenly struck by the urge to don paisley ascots and crank up the Cat Stevens. We found out later that the Elqui Valley was a Chilean hippie holdout in the 1960s, full of wandering wayfarers and neo-yogis. Cool, man! And it's the cooler clime that contributes to this Syrah's elegant characteristics: plush and velvety across the taste buds, but with meaty and peppery qualities found in more austere bottles. Far out and, above all, a fantastic Syrah.

tongue

gyros

wine geek, romance

CHONO
RESERVA
Syrah
14.5% alc./vol. Elqui Valley - 2006 750 ml
Wine - Product of Chile / Vin - Produit du Chili

2006
Syrah
"Reserva"
$17.99

delas

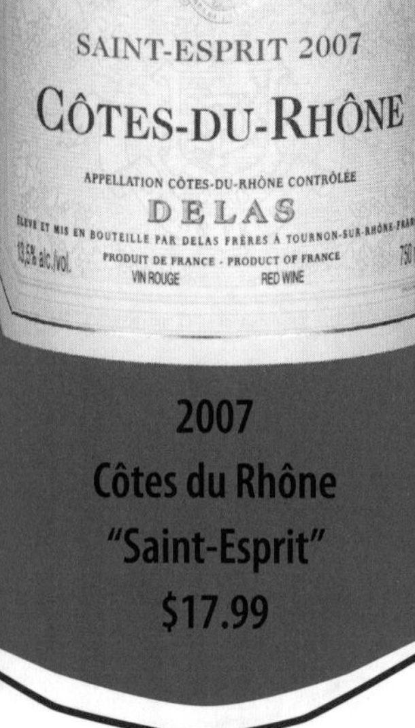

2007
Côtes du Rhône
"Saint-Esprit"
$17.99

We wish we had a yen, an RMB, or a rupee

for every time we've heard that the ideal liquid match to Asian food is an aromatic white. We're not saying a Gewürz or Riesling won't complement your satay or fried rice, but don't overlook *red* wine. We realized this at a sushi bar in a tiny town northwest of Tokyo where we had a 12-month barrel-aged red with monkfish liver sushi. A genius match. Not that you're having monkfish liver tonight, but our point is: Red wine and Asian food might seem unexpected, but once you digest the concept, a new universe is at your fingertips.

spareribs in black bean sauce

romance

Spain | < $20

glorioso

It's back. Glorioso Rioja returns to the pages of *Had a Glass* for the simple reason that it continues to offer fantastic, honest Rioja style at one of the lowest price points in its section at the liquor store. It's "old meets new" in this cherry-chocolate, toasty-cigar-box-and-licorice, 100-percent Tempranillo, with lots of bright fruit, a bold oaky core, and dry tannins to finish. If you're looking to keep it real in red, there's no need to look further.

roast leg

aged and hard

beginner, Wednesday wine

2005
Rioja
"Crianza"
$17.99

< $20 | France

rémy pannier

Cabernet Franc is planted the world over. But, as a single varietal, where do we like it from? The Loire! Alongside its Sauvignon and Merlot brethren, and planted often in really hot zones, it can happen that Franc chunks out. But when it's a Loire libation from a tempered clime, you get the gorgeous tealeaf and raspberry effects that make it such a pleasure to sniff. Pannier's is a perfect intro to the region, to the variety, and to generally great sipping.

curry chicken

seafood bouillabaisse

beginner

2006
Chinon
$17.99

Chile | < $20

cousiño macul

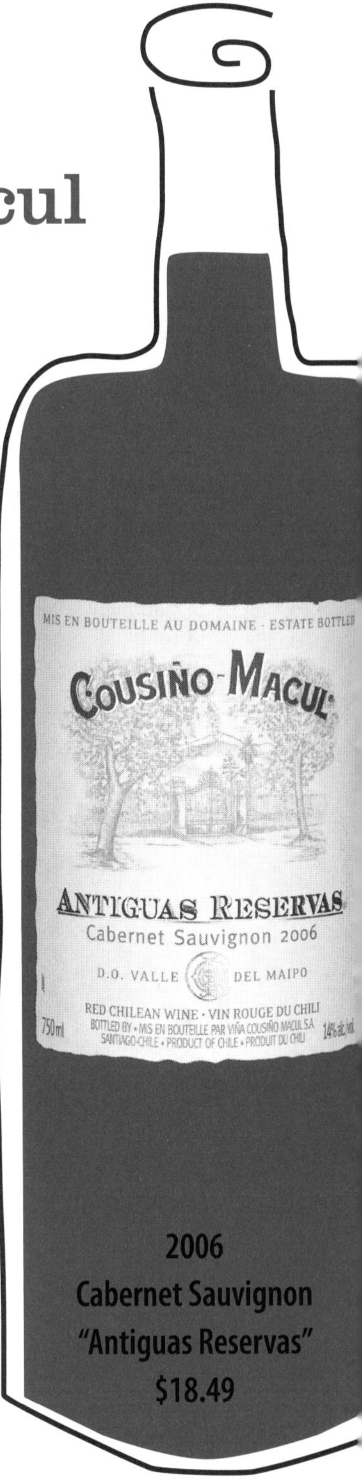

Finally! A wine to pair with suburban sprawl.

The vines of Cousiño Macul, one of Chile's most historic wineries, have watched the metropolis of Santiago grow up around them. Nowadays, public bus #210 from the centre of the city will get you within walking distance of the winery gate—the top of the list of cool ways to arrive for a winery tour. If Santiago's a little far, take TransLink to your local bottle shop to pick up Cousiño Macul's elegant, complex Cab Sauv, a gutsy blackcurrant and wood spice affair.

steak tacos

hard

cellar, wine geek

2006
Cabernet Sauvignon
"Antiguas Reservas"
$18.49

< $20 | British Columbia 

red rooster

We wish we could write HAG while living on a secluded island. No electricity, no phone, no emails. We could get our inspiration from the sound of the waves or a seashell we found on the beach. Or some moss we saw on a tree. The problem with this fantasy is there's a desperate lack of wine on a secluded island. But if we could choose one endlessly quaffable Merlot to take with us, Red Rooster's would be it. Smoky plum, bramble, and vanilla combine to make a fine, endlessly quaffable drink that you can take on any exile from civilization.

2007
Merlot
$18.99

on its own

Saint-Nectaire

beginner

France | < $20

jean-luc colombo

Tasting like a pro means spitting like a pro. That is, spitting out obscure wine adjectives to the chagrin of the poor, unsuspecting public and the mirthful delight of other adjective-spitting wine pros. But which words can take you to pro heights? If you're still on the "oaky" and the "sandpaper tannins," then it's time to step up to "garrigue." We're talking the scrub brush of the Mediterranean in a glass of wine, like this JL Colombo.

stew

Beaufort

BYO

2005
Côtes du Rhône
"Les Abeilles"
$19.96

< $20 | Argentina

amalaya de colomé

Some wines bring a treble kick of acidity. Others riff off a fat melody of smooth, silky fruit. Still others get as floral as flowery power pop. We'll take them all, but man oh man how we love that bass slap and velvet. And when the night is lingering on, winter surrounds, and we need to think of someplace warm, we'll cue up Haruomi Hosono's "Hurricane Dorothy" on the playlist and pop the cork on this Colomé. This smoothie blends Malbec with Cab Sauv, Syrah, Tannat, and Bonarda, and is ready to sashay with soothing rich plum and supple raspberry, capped by a fresh, vanilla-infused finish.

2006
Vino Tinto
$19.99

sticky ribs

winter warmer, patio/picnic

Australia | < $20

cat amongst the pigeons

Just as there's more than one way to skin a cat, there's more than one way to aerate a wine. It's all about getting some softening oxygen mixed into that brutal rouge to tame it to drinkability. We've borne witness to the blender method (the purée setting seems to work best). The partial bottle method (pour a glass, cover the neck of the bottle with your thumb, shake). The fitness method (empty wine into water bottle, go jogging). To crack this bottle of monster Shiraz and release its ripe blueberry and cracked pepper, we went for the daredevil method: think scissor lift and a pail. Do not try this at home!

on its own

cellar

2006
Shiraz
"Nine Lives"
$19.99

chapoutier

An ode to Rasteau:

There is a red wine from Rasteau,
Produced by an honoured château.
Full with black cherry,
We drank and were merry,
The next morning our heads were aglow.

rack

satay

wine geek,
rock out

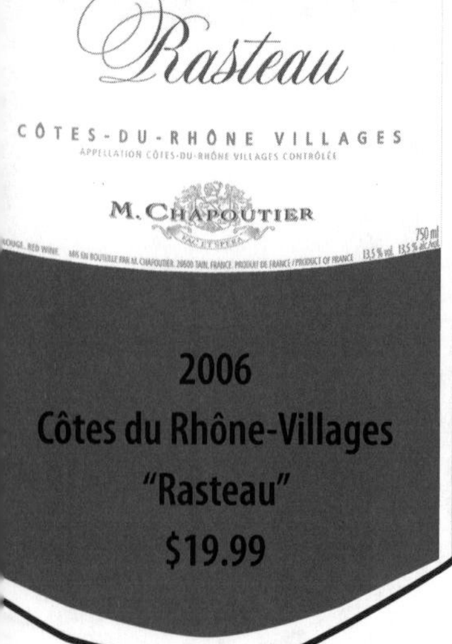

2006
Côtes du Rhône-Villages
"Rasteau"
$19.99

South Africa | < $20

graham beck

We met the eponymous gamekeeper. His name is Mossie Basson. He takes care of the winery's game reserve. We had a *braai*—a South African tradition—what we in North America would call a barbecue. Or BBQ. At a *braai*, one person is always in charge. Mossie braaied a *snoek* (pronounced *snook*). A *snoek* is what we in North America would call a snook. It's a fish. When the *snoek* was on the *braai*, Mossie basted it with apricot jam.

BBQ

winter warmer

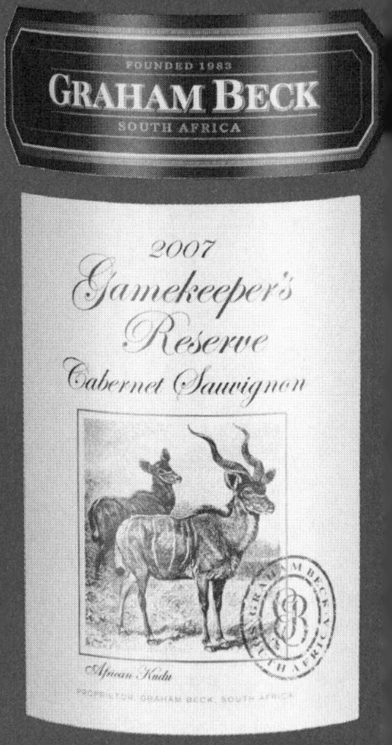

2007
Cabernet Sauvignon
"Gamekeeper's Reserve"
$19.99

Our tastes change. You know what we're talking about. There was a time when we all wore Vans and listened to GnR. Then it was baggy jeans and sliding cassette tapes of Public Enemy into our Walkmans. The millennium rang in retro, and when we weren't at a Weezer show we were in the thrift shop. But our taste for Masi's SA never changed. We loved this wine years ago. We love it now. In fact, just the other day we were finishing off a bottle, tapping our Sk8-Hi's and racing each other on Burnout Paradise.

lasagna

aged Cheddar

rock out, patio/picnic

2006
Veronese
"Serego Alighieri"
$19.99

Australia | < $20

penfolds

We like a wine that sticks to the ribs. A wine that puts hair on the chest. Which calls for a gutsy red or white. Not some overripe fruit shysters or winery-manipulated tricksters that hide behind over-extraction and over-oak. We want true, bold provocateurs! The T. Hyland Shiraz, thankfully, is the real deal. It's heavy, dense with plum, leather, and no shortage of charred, vanilla-scented oak, but the fruit has quality that holds its own.

roast

burgers

BYO, beginner

2005
Shiraz
"Thomas Hyland"
$19.99

viu manent

Lean times call for voluptuous wines. So there's nothing wrong with squeezing extra pleasure out of the bottle. Giving your palate over to unrestrained hedonism. Take ripe grapes from Chile's hot, hot Colchagua Valley, massage them in French oak barrels, and—when handled with loving care—here's your end result: a sumptuous symphony of coffee beans, eucalyptus, herbs, and ripe figs. Rich enough to assuage a wary soul and with enough structure to appease worried taste buds.

duck confit

rock out

2006
Cabernet Sauvignon
"Reserva"
$19.99

Greece | < $25

notios

Agiorgitiko is quite possibly the most syllabic of grape varieties, though Huxelrebe and Mtsvane come pretty close. And when made well, ah-yor-YEE-ti-ko is an indigenous Greek standout. Notios has "done good" with this hearty red from the Nemea region of the Peloponnese. It offers up ample ripe plum and raspberry before finishing with a refreshingly prickly finish.

souvlaki

roast shoulder

patio/picnic, wine geek

2006
Agiorgitiko
$21.30

< $25 | Italy 

ceuso scurati

THIS is why it's exciting to drink wine.

Forget the hype! Forget the buzz! The Scurati represents all that is good about vino. You could pay twice the price for a bottle and still not find this much flavour, class, and complexity. Rich, sumptuous blackberry, cassis, and anise are the stars in this heady, full-on bottle made from 100 percent Nero d'Avola. Run, don't walk, to go grab this bottle and uncork the excitement.

braised short ribs

hush puppies

winter warmer, rock out

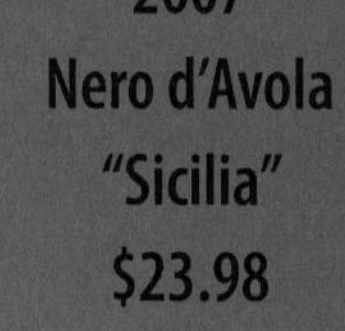

2007
Nero d'Avola
"Sicilia"
$23.98

France | < $25

plan de dieu

There's a hiccup in the Had a Glass price-value continuum. Past theories reported that value decreases as price increases, in a proportional, Euclidean manner. But as we sip wine close to the speed of light, Gratitude appears on the oenophilic radar, and all classical ideas about price value, about big bang for your buck—heck, even about space-time—get efficiently put through the proverbial shredder. The zenith of value in the upper price echelon, here is bottled proof that, occasionally, paying a little bit extra can blow your socks off tenfold.

shanks

chili

wine geek

2007
Côtes du Rhône-Villages
"Gratitude"
$23.99

château sainte-eulalie

Usually it's not the size of the wine that matters. It's how well balanced it is. But when it comes to the Ch. Sainte-Eulalie's Minervois, this powerhouse red from the south of France comes decked out with an arresting concentration of plum, sage, and tar. It's supple but still has a poise usually reserved for runway models. Suddenly, we have both kick and chic in the same glass.

brisket

Moroccan-spiced chops

rock out, BYO

2006
Minervois la Livinière
"La Cantilène"
$24.99

Washington | < $25

desert wind

When you bring together the Bordeaux triumvirate of CS, CF, and M, things can go very well. Should the stars, planets, and Coco Crisp's ball cap align, things can go so fantastically perfect—a mind meld of the best in the business—like this Ruah. The details of the mix aren't relevant; it's the pencil-lead, mint, and tobacco touches that stand out as hallmarks of the blend. The balance and the structure are in perfect tune. If your cellar isn't stocked with Ruah, you might as well rent it out as a basement suite.

roast

cellar, wine geek

2006
Cabernet Franc/Cabernet Sauvignon/Merlot
"Ruah"
$24.99

quails' gate

Quails' Gate cooks up some real-deal red for those Pinot-philes among you who like a heartbreak grape made to spec. No fooling around with Petite Sirah to ramp up the colour. No over-toasted two-by-fours to inject that vanilla cornball. No super-extraction. No jam jar. This is a straight shooter: Pinot-busting cherry kicks and leafy leaf. Silky and fresh like a good fantasy.

mushroom bruschetta

BBQ duck

wine geek

2007
Pinot Noir
$24.99

British Columbia | < $25

road 13

The winery formerly known as Golden Mile Cellars checked in for a makeover. What emerged from the flames of rebranding was the slicked-out Road 13. But style is only label-deep. What hasn't changed is their vineyard panache and fine winemaking. Or perhaps the fineness is getting even finer. This finger-licking Shiraz is a prime example of deliciousness from our own backyard, with bacon and blueberry framed by beguiling aromatics.

goulash

fungi pizza

winter warmer

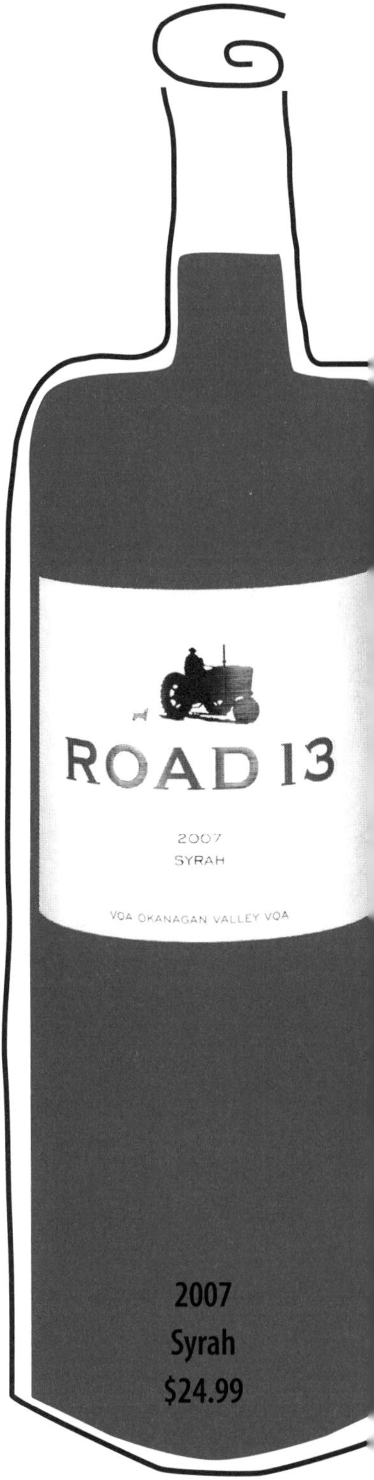

2007
Syrah
$24.99

blasted church vineyards

If grapes were Japanese feudal warriors, Merlot would be a ronin. Like the seventh of the seven samurais, the variety fallen from public favour would roam the countryside masterless, with mutable temperament, only surfacing to unpredictable consequence. Unless it rose from the cellars of Blasted Church. Here the grape has guidance: its potential is tapped to its fullest plum and chocolate savour—stark, well structured, and busting heads.

T-bone

winter warmer

2007
Merlot
$25.90

Australia | < $30

serafino

There are two kinds of wine festivals in this world. One is where the wine comes to you. You stroll around the aisles of some convention centre, glass in hand, smiling at other wine geeks, taking a slurp here and a slurp there from the vendors' booths as you register your notes in your tasting book. Then there is the kind of wine festival they have in the McLaren Vale, where every winery in spitting distance has its cellar door open and wines on tap. First, you're on foot and for good reason. Second, who cares about wine glasses? Third, you pass out in a field.

steak pizza

grilled rack, mustard marinade

BYO

2006
Shiraz
$26.00

< $30 | Argentina 

clos de los siete

Wine haiku:

Ah, Michel Rolland

You are controversial

But your wine's tasty.

BBQ

romance, rock out

2007
Malbec/Merlot/Syrah/
Cabernet Sauvignon
$26.89

Australia | < $30

cape jaffa

This Shiraz is one of the best we sipped all year. Not because the grapes for this wine were grown following biodynamic principles (even though they were). Not because it comes from the less-advertised but hugely promising region of Mount Benson on the Limestone Coast (which it does). Not because the fruit is painstakingly estate grown (which it is). And not because the label may be capable of channelling cosmic energy (still under investigation). This is incredible wine simply because it tastes incredibly good.

pork and beans

Cantal

cellar, rock out

2006
Shiraz
$26.99

rabbit ranch

2007
Pinot Noir
$26.99

What's so great about off-off-Broadway wine growing? Well, we can taste along latitudes and in and out of hemispheres and discover that some of the world's greatest wines come from regions that are *on the edge*. Places where vines struggle because of cold, humidity, lack of rainfall, or some other objectionable condition. Central Otago is out there, waaaay on the fringes of New Zealand's South Island. The region is not your cordial Marlborough (the capital of Sauvignon Blanc) or affable Hawkes Bay (Chardonnay country). This cherry Coke and leaf-pile Pinot, challenged by savage altitudinal temperature swings, high winds, and cold winters, is about as "outer frontier" as you get.

tuna tataki, pan-fried sockeye

BYO, romance

 British Columbia | < $30

tinhorn creek

A screw cap story: When Tinhorn Creek first released their premium bottling of Merlot back in 2001, they ran an experiment. Not an in-house experiment restricted for the lab rats, but an experiment that the fine-wine-drinking public could get into. When you bought your two-pack of OC Merlot, one was closed with a cork, and the other with a screw cap. We recently tried the original vintage back-to-back, and, seven years later, the cork-closed wine was just demonstrating its peak, but the screw-capped version was still vibrant and fresh and ready for another five years in the cellar. Is there a right answer? Suffice it to say, the newer releases, including this one, are all under "cap."

 braised short ribs

 wine geek

2005
Merlot
"Oldfield's Collection"
$28.00

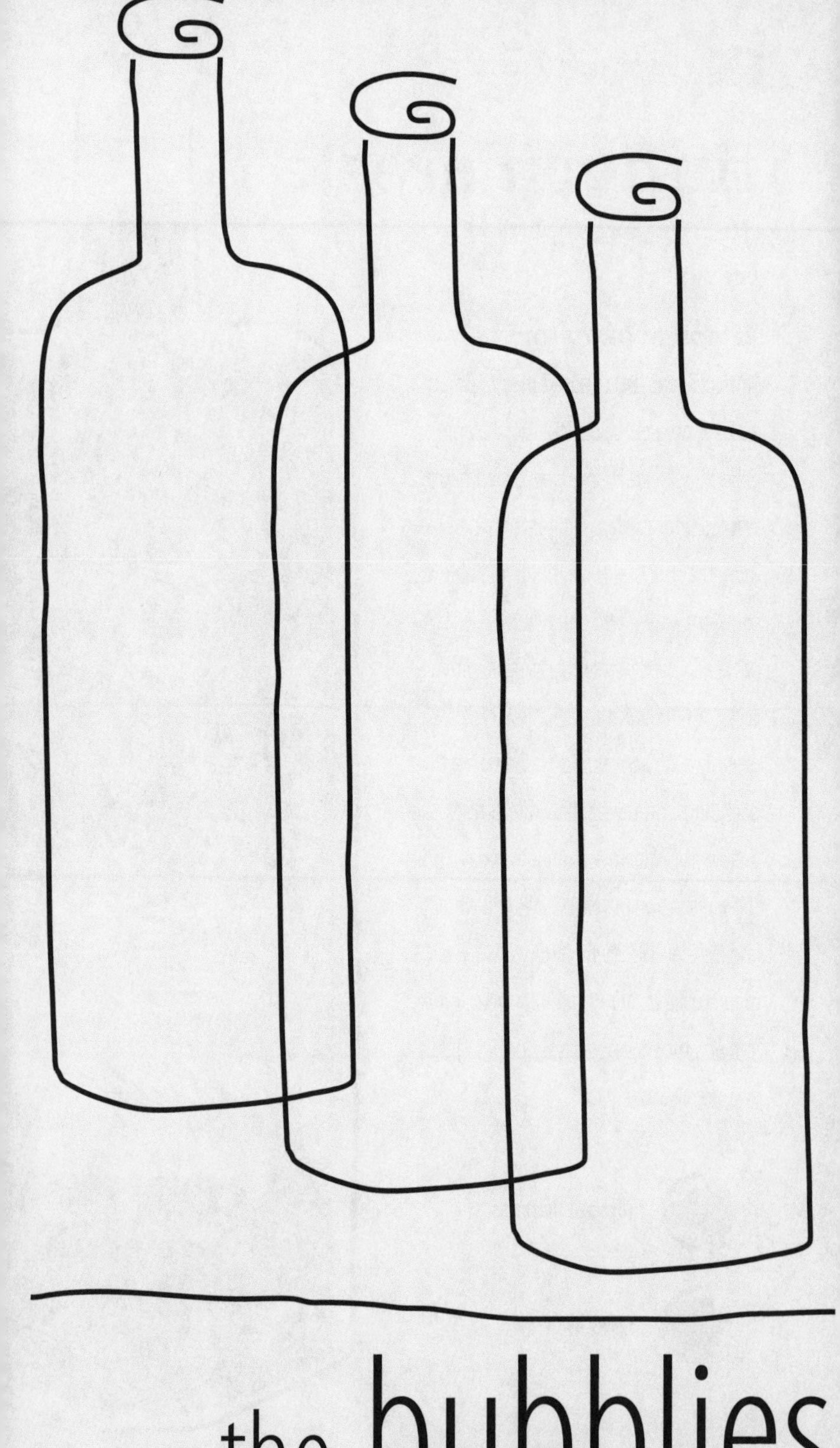

the bubblies

Hungary | < $20

hungaria

"Pop corks of the best grapes. Make the best CDs and the best tapes."

Biggie Smalls may have preferred to sip Champagne, but we bet he still stepped down to have a glass of traditional method once in a while. And when he did, we bet his was a bottle of Hungaria. Why? Because it's so Champagne and so damn cheap. Plus, East Coast reps Eastern Europe to the fullest. Rest in peace, Notorious B.I.G. Toss on *Life After Death*, pop the cork on a bottle of Hungaria, and you'll be amazed at how easy the evening flows. This is a fridge stocker. Our flirtation with Cava notwithstanding, it has become our go-to everyday sparkler.

lobster thermidor

BYO, Wednesday wine

Brut
"Grande Cuvée"
$13.90

< $20 | Spain 

codorníu

On a lark in a French bistro, we ordered a bottle of Codorníu Clasico. There were some real Champagnes on the menu, but the wine alone would have eclipsed the investment in our casual fare. Back from the pan-Euro affair, we must report we were gobsmacked with the result. Duck confit and Cava! Sweetbreads and Cava! Cassoulet and Cava! Even the moules frites matched up great with the CC's toasty aromas and apple, pear, and lime-rind twang of a finish. More Cava, please!

duck confit

moules mariniere

Wednesday wine, patio/picnic

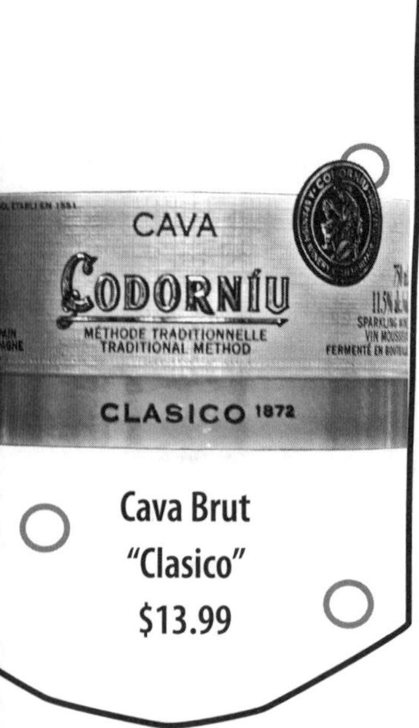

Cava Brut "Clasico" $13.99

Italy | < $25

mionetto

We were at a wine tasting not too long ago, a late-afternoon event where the room was dotted with tables, at each table a bottle of wine and the wine's rep. It was a good vibe: a little house music, some eats, and lots of vino. Anyway, we're chatting with the guy who's pouring this Mionetto just before the end of the tasting. Suddenly a very fine-looking and well-dressed group of women materialize from the horde. Glasses in hand and grinning, they say in near chorus, "We deliberately saved this wine for last!" Ah, the magic of great bubble.

on its own

crab

aperitif, romanc

Frizzante
Prosecco di Valdobbiadene
$21.99

freixenet

The magnum has its purpose(s). Some people like them for the stature they add to their wine collection. Some like them for their prowess in the cellar; how they help slow a wine's aging. Some like them because they are rare and make for a solid wine investment. Our magnum purpose is PARTY. Show up at the party toting a magnum of sparkling wine, and you're a star. We opt for the Cordon Negro. Not only is it large and in charge, it won't break the bank. Plus, this black beauty is an imminently sippable sparkler, showing smooth citrus and pear that finishes nice and crisp.

Cava Brut
"Cordon Negro"
$28.99 for 1.5 L

nachos

bacon sarnies

rock out, BYO

California | < $30

gloria ferrer

As we expand the price point up to $30 this year, we allow ourselves to explore some finer points on wine, but more specifically—and more merrily—the finer points on bubble. Bubble isn't always the most price-accommodating bevvie because of its labour-intensive creation. Not to mention that big-C Champagne, despite an irrevocably characteristic charm, has caused more than one eyebrow to raise over the high entry price (we couldn't even get a half bottle of the stuff in this book). But Gloria splits it down the middle: Champagne-esque for half the price. What more can you ask for?

egg salad sandwich

aperitif, romance

Brut
$29.99

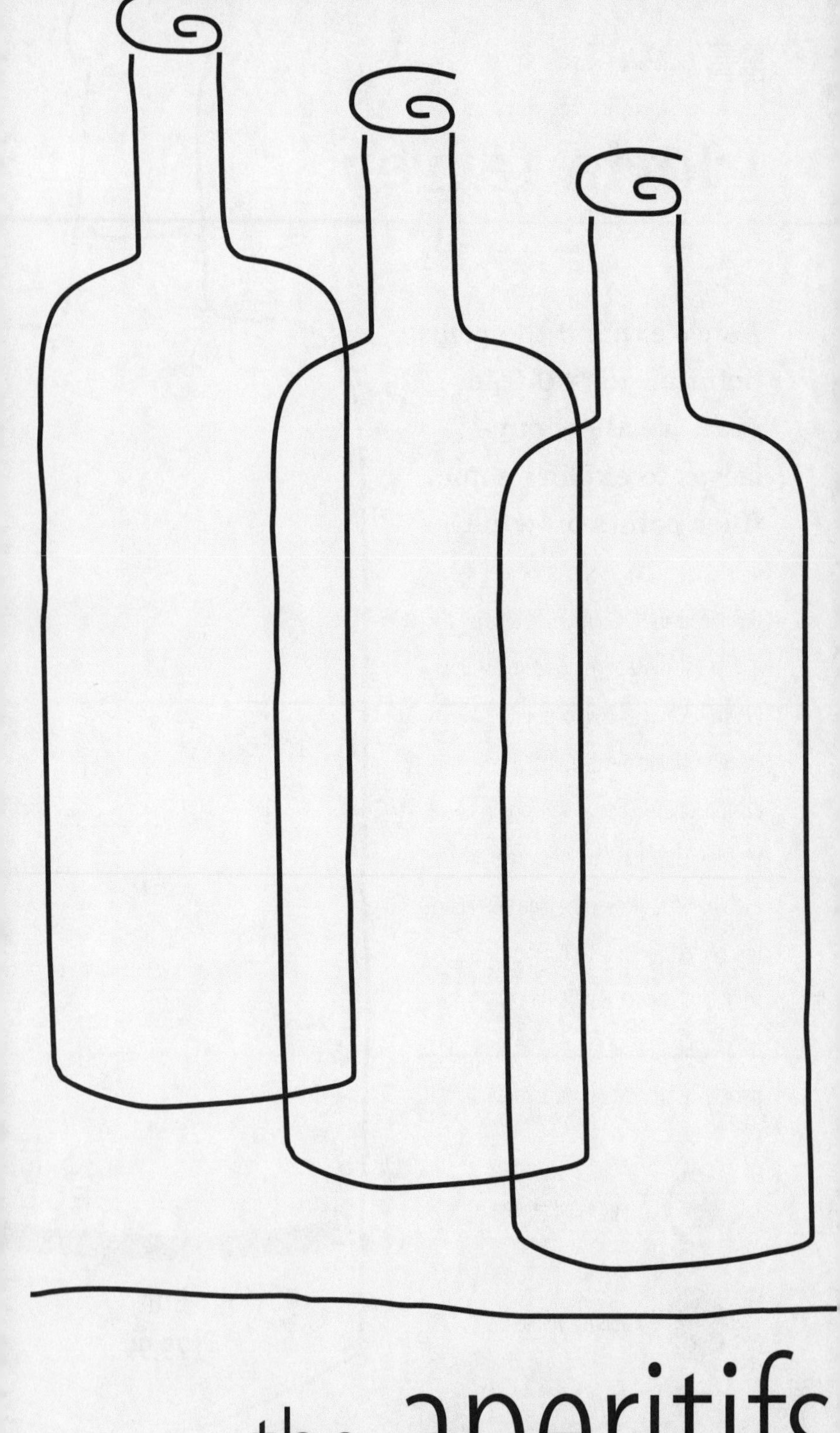

the aperitifs

France | < $20

noilly prat

Like its sweeter brethren on page 152, Noilly is a fantastic pre-dinner play. Follow the instructions listed under the Cinzano for simple aperitif bliss (simply chilled with a lemon twist), or tag-team the vermouths in that classic Canuck cocktail, the Manhattan Perfect: 1½ ounces of rye (only Canadian will do!), ½ ounce each of dry and sweet vermouths, a couple dashes of bitters, and a brandied cherry for garnish. In 2010, it's time to have both vermouths, dry and sweet, at the ready.

on its own

bowl of pistachios

Wednesday wine, patio/picnic

Vermouth
"Extra Dry"
$11.99 for 1 L

cinzano

Vermouth gets the gut grooving! Too often it gets tossed into the murky depths of a cocktail shaker. While there's no doubt vermouth is integral to many a mean mixed drink, it holds its own as a top-notch aperitif. Keep a bottle of Cinzano in the door of the fridge, and an hour before dinner, pour a jigger into a wine glass and twist in a lemon peel for a magically herbal, coriander-and-camomile, citrus-lifted libation reminiscent of an apothecary. For those that find the straight goods a little too strong, top it up with a splash of club soda.

on its own

jerky

BYO, winter warmer

Vermouth
"Rosso"
$12.75 for 1 L

France | < $25

marnier lapostolle

While the label tells us to serve this as an aperitif, we have to admit we're not fully on board. What we are on board with is the incredibly concentrated flavours of slightly oxidative apricot, nuts, orange peel, and spice that go down just a little too easy. The commune of Cognac might hang us, but we like this as a dessert bevvie. But before dinner, after dinner—hell, even during dinner—this bottle sits in our fridge door and calls to us. It knows our names.

on its own

rock out

Pineau des Charentes
$21.55

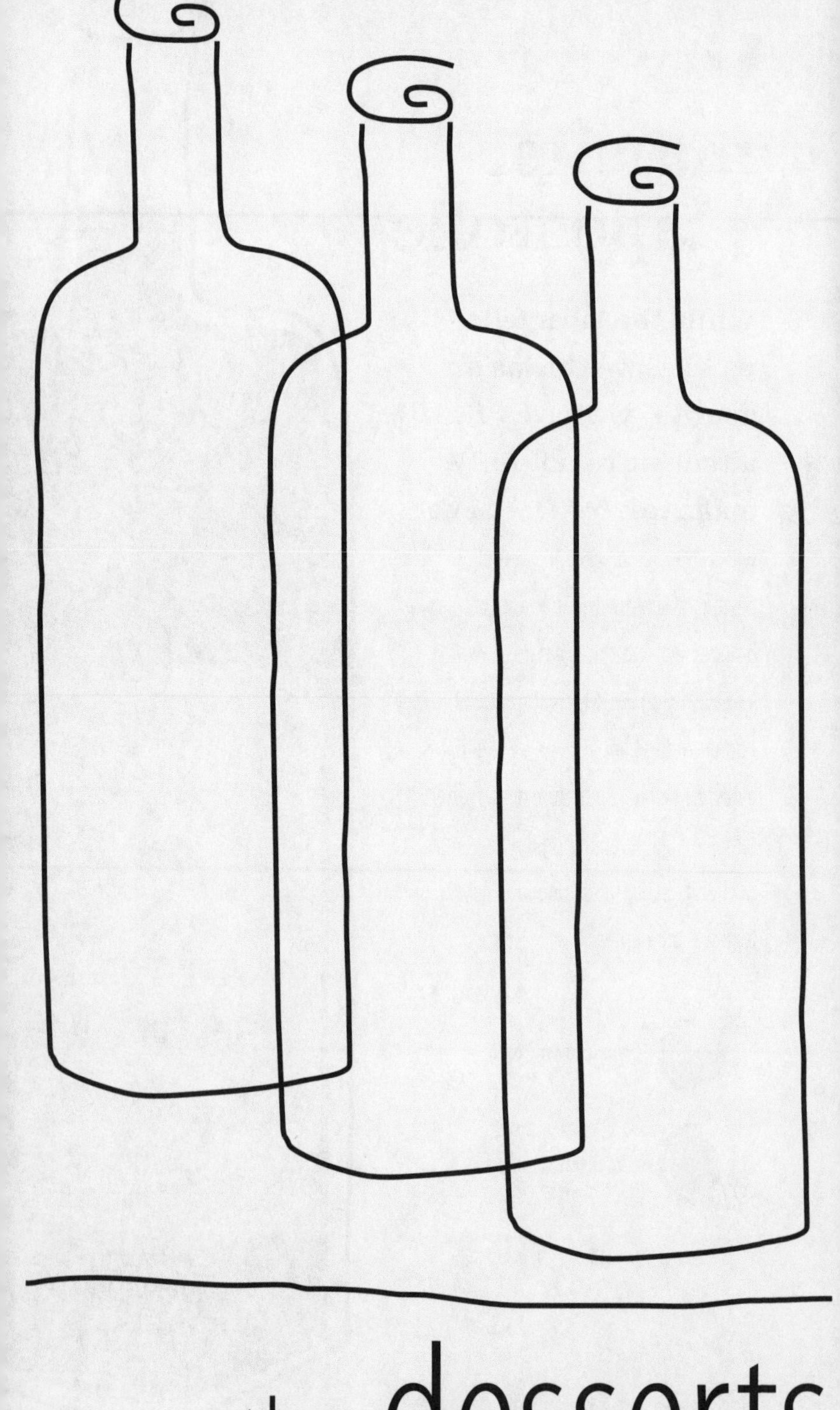

the desserts

Chile | < $20

concha y toro

Nothing beats the smell of noble rot in the spring. Or in summer, fall, or winter, for that matter. Intuitively, mould and decay shouldn't be so appealing, but *Botrytis cinerea*, or noble rot, is one funky, fun-loving fungus. It attacks bunches of grapes hanging long on the vines, sucking out their moisture, and, when conditions are right, concentrates the sugars and fruit flavours. With this LH Sauv Blanc, the lip-smacking end result is a jaw-dropping combo of pure honeyed apricot, tangerine, and lime-rind goodness in the glass.

blue

romance, wine geek

2005
Late Harvest
Sauvignon Blanc
"Private Reserve"
$14.98 for 375 mL

elephant island

2008
Framboise
$19.90 for 375 mL

Fruit wines are the alternative wines of the wine world. It's like psychobilly when everyone's listening to country. Like Melt Banana when everyone's listening to Sufjan Stevens. Like B-boy when everyone's head's banging. OK, maybe cardboard and duct tape at a metal show doesn't go over so well, but fruit wines stay unique and still give you the buzz. El's Framboise (that's raspberry, folks) just gets better and better every year. We can't understand how so much flavour can get stuffed into one bottle, but, frankly, it's a mystery we're willing to let live.

on its own

chocolate cake, with ice cream

romance

Portugal | < $30

dow’s

Anytime we’re feeling a little Kerouac, or just a little beat, we reach for the port. But not any port. Just because port is hopped up on distilled alcohol to 20 percent and flaunts around 130 g/L of sugar (like a bowl of Froot Loops in every glass) it doesn’t mean that we need to be nonchalant about what kind of wine we place beside the Underwood. Make it tasty! The Dow’s is an arrestingly delicious port, and it won’t shock your wallet. It’s the real deal: ripe plums, cherry compote, and chocolate. Where’s the poetry reading?

walnuts

manchego

winter warmer

2003
Port
Late Bottled Vintage
$25.99

hardys

When she tossed the Fleetwood Mac on the turntable, I knew I was in trouble. After a few seconds of warm crackle and pop, on came those welcoming guitar licks. When she poured me a few fingers of Whiskers Tawny, there was no turning back. A multitude of candied orange peel, hazelnut, red licorice, and toffee flavours cascaded lovingly down my gullet as Stevie crescendoed, " . . . landslide."

on its own

Parmigiano

romance

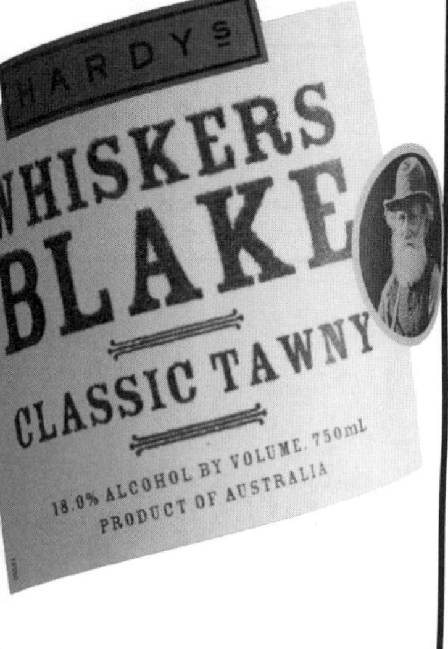

Classic Tawny "Whiskers Blake" $25.99

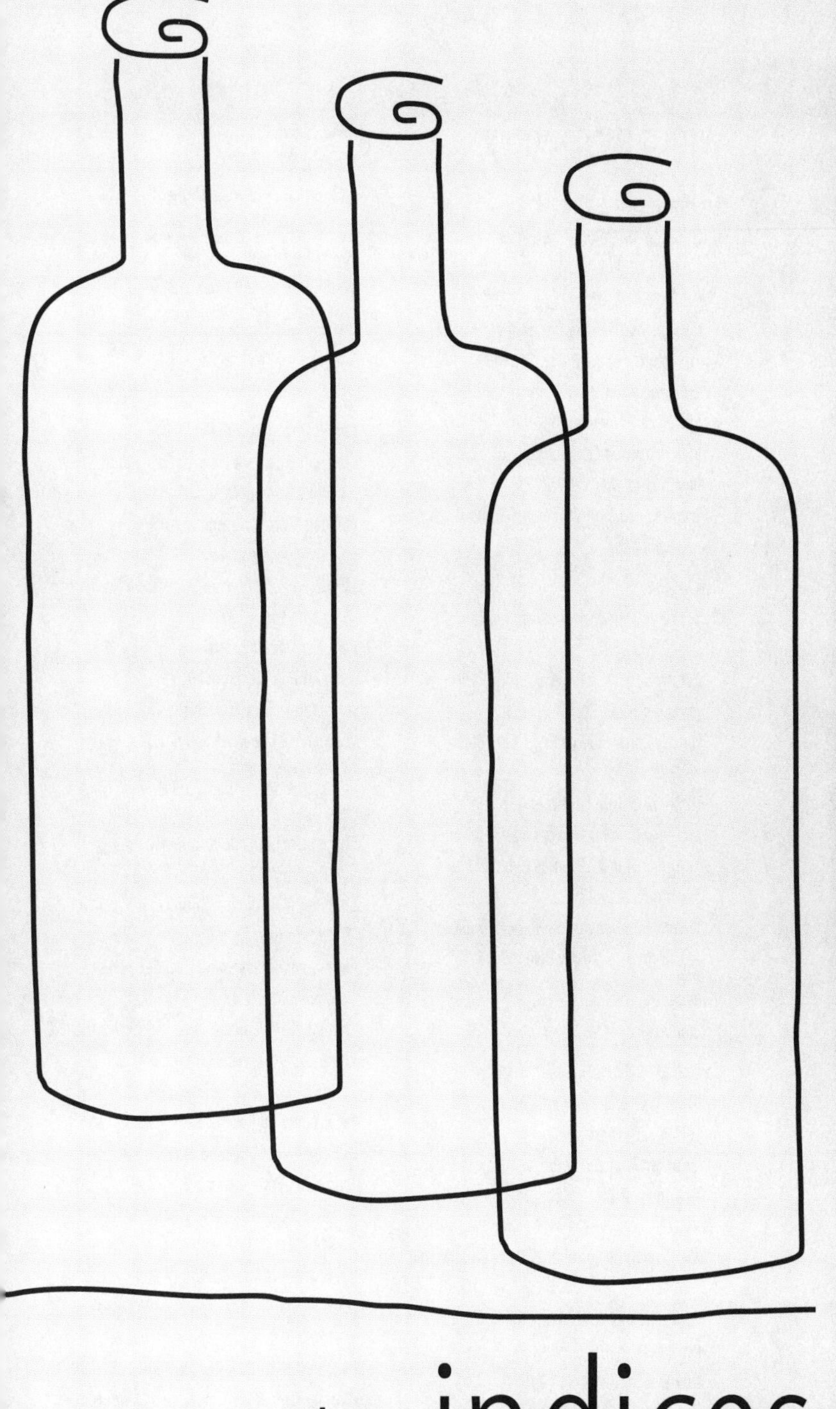

the indices

wines by country

Argentina

Australia

Austria

Canada—British Columbia

Canada—Ontario

Chile

France

wines by type

wines by food

Finally, *gros bisous* to our families and friends for their [e]ndless encouragement. And not least to Karen and Mai: We [p]romise that the tasting glasses are being retired for the night [a]nd that the computer is getting powered down.

Now turn back to page 119 and try that Rioja already!

acknowledgements

Five years ago, when we compiled our Top 100 valı the first time, we didn't envision that this book woı an annual endeavour. Thanks to your support anc thirst we have a new 100 for 2010. We'd like to raise to everyone who has leafed through an edition of maybe even spilled some Syrah on it in the prı your wine adventures continue.

None of this would be possible without Rob great crew at Whitecap Books. The amount of edit ing, photographing—not to mention carting w around—that is required to complete a project *Glass* is no small matter; a sincere thank you, salı cin cin goes to everyone that contributed.

Extra appreciation must also be extended to (co-conspirators who generously donated their recipes) to the *Had a Glass* cause. The good life is tı ied by simply conversing with good people over and good food. This year, thanks to the people iı pages speak directly to this cause.

We would also like to acknowledge the wineı and wine shops that are passionate about bringinç wines to market. There is nothing more exciting bling across the next great wine that pleases the so please keep expanding our wine horizons (and

Thank you also to the venues that continue column space for our wine musings, namely t newspaper, *Wine Access*, and *TASTE* magazine.